ISLE OF ELY

The Washes

Bedford River

New Bedford River

A1123

Haddenham

Wilburton

Streetham

Aldreth

A10

SOHAM MERE

SOHAM

A1123

TO MILDENHALL

Great Ouse (Old West River)

TWENTY PENCE BRIDGE

Setchel Road

Streatham Mere

WICKEN FEN

HEMPSALS FEN

SMITHEY FEN

SETCHEL FEN

Twenty Pence Road

NORTH FEN

ADVENTURERS' FEN

JOLLY WATERMAN

COTTENHAM CHURCH

THREE HORSESHOES

DENNY ABBEY

Upware

Reach Lode

BURWELL

Rampton

Cottenham

MASON'S PASTURES or COTTENHAM RACECOURSE

AIRFIELD

SWAFFHAM PRIOR FEN

Reach

TO NORWICH & BURY

Longstanton

Waterbeach

River Cam

BOTTISHAM FEN

Swaffham Prior

A11

NEWMARKET

AIRFIELD

Oakington

Landbeach

OUY FEN

Swaffham Bulbeck

RACECOURSE

Devil's Dyke

CHIVERS FACTORY

Milton

Horningsea

Lode

HALL

A45

Girton

Histon & Impington

Stow cum Quay

Bottisham

GIRTON COLLEGE

UNIVERSITY PITT CLUB

Chesterton

MAGDALENE COLLEGE

Little Wilbraham

OLD OBSERVATORY SITE

Fen Ditton

Coton

CAMBRIDGE

TEVERSHAM and FULBOURN FENS

Great Wilbraham

TRINITY COLLEGE BACKS

CHERRY HINTON

Grantchester

HALL

FULBOURN

A11

Trumpington

Gog Magog Hills

Fleam Dyke

GREAT BRADLEY HALL

or Rhee

The Shelfords

River Cam or Granta

Hauxton

Newton

HALL

SAWSTON

The Abingdons

STREETLY HALL

Wittlesford

LINTON

Horseheath

Fowlmere

A505

Duxford

Stump Cross

A604 TO HAVERHILL & COLCHESTER

ESSEX

A130 TO SAFFRON WALDEN

HERTFORDSHIRE

THE TRINITY FOOT BEAGLES

THE TRINITY FOOT BEAGLES

A history of the pack and a description of
the Sporting Cantab
with appendices on the Cambridge University Drag Hounds
and the Whip Club

JAMES KNOX

J. A. ALLEN
London & New York

British Library Cataloguing in Publication Data

Knox, James
   History of the Trinity Foot Beagles.
   1. Trinity Foot Beagles (club) – History
   I. Title
   799.2'34   SK186.C

   ISBN 0-85131-309-4

Published in Great Britain in 1980 by
J. A. Allen & Company Limited,
1, Lower Grosvenor Place, Buckingham Palace Road,
London, SW1W 0EL
and in the United States of America by
Sporting Book Center, Inc.,
Canaan, N.Y. 12029.

Book design by Bill Ireson.
Typeset, Compugraphic 11/13 Bembo, by Computacomp (UK) Limited,
Fort William, Scotland.
Printed in Great Britain by St Edmundsbury Press, Bury St Edmunds, Suffolk.
Bound by J. M. Dent & Sons Limited, Letchworth.

Dedicated to
Charles Smyth-Osbourne and Henry Fayre
present masters of the Trinity Foot Beagles
and to their successors

CONTENTS

Group photograph taken on Trinity College Backs in 1912, the year the first TFB history was published. The master (*centre*) is I.A. Straker. The two whips on either side of him are W.P.D. Clarke (*left*) and G.W. Barclay (*right*). Barclay who succeeded as master in 1912 was later one of the many TFB casualties in the First World War. Bob Floate, senior, stands on the far right.

ACKNOWLEDGEMENTS

The author is grateful to the following for permission to reproduce illustrations (bracketed numbers indicate page in the book): Tryon Gallery (frontispiece); Prudence Cumming Associates (8/9; 25; 28; 30; 74; 75; 81 and 96); *Cambridge Daily News* (26; 40/41; 88/89); W. Eaden Lilley (112). All other illustrations were supplied from the author's collection. The endpaper was created by Logo Design from an original drawing by Jon Harris.

LIST OF ILLUSTRATIONS

INTRODUCTION

The first history of the Trinity Foot Beagles came out in 1912. [*The Trinity Foot Beagles, 1862–1912*. F. Claude Kempson, M.A., published by Edward Arnold.] It had been conceived two years earlier by the Reverend F.C. Kempson and one of the most famous masters of the pack T. Holland-Hibbert, when they were descending Castle Hill on the box seat of the beagle brake after a day in the fens. F.C. Kempson volunteered to write the history because he had already qualified as an author with one serious work entitled *Oarsmanship and Training* and two lighthearted volumes on his experiences as a sailor.

His history of the TFB is an admirable work of reference. It consists of letters written by early masters recalling their hunting experiences whilst up at Cambridge. Kempson intersperses these reminiscences with thoughts of his own on both hunting and life in general. The book never received the recognition it deserved for F.C. Kempson, with his monocle and double chins, was considered rather a joke by undergraduates. Indeed survivors from this period still mischievously suggest that he had been defrocked.

In fact he led a blameless life. First as an undergraduate of Gonville and Caius where he read medicine, and then, on going down in 1895, when he entered the church as deacon of St. Mary the Less in Trumpington Street. On being ordained he became parson of St. Luke's, New Chesterton and later moved to the parish of Nether Dean in Bedfordshire. Apart from his ecclesiastical career, he also pursued that of Demonstrator of Anatomy in the University of Cambridge. As recreation he coached eights on the river, which explains his book on oarsmanship and training.

In 1910 he moved to the remote fen parish on Manea, near March. There he gave a meet for the TFB at the vicarage and so came into contact with the pack for the first time. From that moment he became a keen follower, arranging meets for them in his parish and occasionally attending beagle dinners as a guest. After the First World War he left Cambridgeshire for the West Country, where he died in 1922.

In writing this present history I have concentrated upon the years from 1912 until the present day, but I have also described the 19th-century origins of the pack. This would have been impossible without the existence of F.C. Kempson's book. I have drawn information from it in the knowledge that it has long been out of print and is extremely scarce. I hope that those readers who are acquainted with it will tolerate my occasional excursions into Mr. Kempson's country.

The oldest member of the hunt to be consulted was the late Mr. Geoffrey Dent, who whipped in to R.S. Clarke during the season 1912–13. When I visited him in 1977 he recalled the names of all his favourite hounds, as well as other details of undergraduate life before the First World War. Having talked well into the night we then went hunting with the Scarsdale Foxhounds the next day. Such a reception was typical of the many I received from ex-TFB men. I would like to thank them all and especially those who lent me their hunting diaries from Cambridge days. The following deserve especial mention: Sir Victor Seely Bt., Colonel W.H. Whitbread, A.F. Goddard-Jackson, Esq., the late Major Robert Hoare, Brandon Cadbury, Esq., the late Major J.J. Mann M.F.H., Captain C.G.E. Barclay M.F.H., Sir John Milburn Bt. M.F.H., Major R.P.G. Dill, J.R. Sclater, Esq., Captain R.M. Festing, Captain N.H. Scott-Barrett, and R.H. Gladstone, Esq.

My father, Colonel B.M. Knox, was up at Cambridge from 1934–1937 and acted as unofficial whip to J.J. Mann. He was the inspiration of the chapter on the war years. I would also like to thank Major-General Viscount Monckton of Brenchley for lending me his diary and newspaper cuttings relating to the Cambridge University Whip Club.

M.I.M. Hutchinson, who was my joint-master of the TFB, was kind enough to drive me round the old haunts in Northumberland. Two people were particularly helpful during this trip; Mrs. Church, daughter of the Reverend R.F. Allgood of Ingram and Mr. Nicholas Beveridge of the Bridge of Aln Hotel. Mr. Beveridge not only provided us with much needed refreshment, but also lent me numerous letters and photographs relating to the TFB's stay at the hotel between the two world wars.

Members of the TFB have been assiduous in compiling official records and minute books. Fortunately most of these have survived and where memory or private diaries have failed, they have proved invaluable. I am grateful to the recent masters for lending me all these books, often for a considerable period of time. I also benefited from a number of earlier attempts to update the history. The first was made by the late William de Geijar a devoted, but mysterious supporter of the TFB, who collected enough information to write a brief pamphlet in 1951. More serious attempts were made at the centenary of the pack in 1962 and again in 1965 and 1973. The letters that resulted from these efforts, and in particular the transcript of Sir Ralph Clarke's hunting diary from 1911–13, were of great assistance.

Finally I would like to thank two people who have provided continuous support throughout the writing of this short history. First Monsignor A.N. Gilbey whose enthusiasm has been unflagging. His knowledge of Cambridge and her personalities, quite apart from the many masters with whom he has hunted, has resulted in many of the more esoteric anecdotes that appear in this book. Certainly without his interest in reading each chapter as it was finished, the book would have taken even longer to write than it did. The second individual who has helped in a different way is Robin Greenwood, Esq. He was master from 1973–75 and is now a trustee of the pack. His reading of the manuscript and his many excellent suggestions lent historical accuracy to an otherwise light-hearted book.

I think F.C. Kempson would be surprised at the publication of another history of the TFB. He wrote his Introduction on the eve of the First World War and finished it with the words: "We are living among changes of which no one knows the end." It is gratifying to think that amidst all those changes the TFB has flourished; that it has continued to cultivate its traditions, and to provide sport for undergraduates. Long may it do so!

CHAPTER ONE

ORIGINS

For centuries the Cantab has spent much of his time at university quenching his thirst for sport. A simple inscription above a staircase entrance in the First Court of St. John's College is striking evidence of this. It reads: "Stag. Novr 15 1777". This refers to an historic day with the Essex Staghounds when Tye, an Irishman of fortune, and commoner of that college accompanied by Lord Euston then an undergraduate at Trinity, and many other members of the university rode hard across the courts of Trinity and St. John's, desecrating the lawns in pursuit of their stag, which they took at the foot of G staircase.

In Regency days undergraduates with sporting inclinations were known as "varmint men". Their activities were varied including racing at Newmarket, fighting the bargees by the river, shooting at Six Mile Bottom and expressing a staunch admiration for the bottle. During this period shooting was plentiful even on the outskirts of Cambridge. Henry Gunning in his *Reminiscences* recalls "how in going over the land now occupied by Downing Terrace, you generally got five or six shots at snipe." The two pursuits abhorrent to them were going to chapel and attending lectures. The next generation were known simply as sporting men. In *Sketches of Cantab* published in 1849 they are described as follows:

> The Sporting Man may be recognised by his having something or other about him, which reminds you forcibly of the stable ... He is much given to huge overcoats, with saucer buttons, and his hat, a very bad one (all sporting men wear bad hats) is secured from being carried off, by means of a string which is attached to one of the button holes. When not actually in his cap and gown, he may be often distinguished from the professional groom by his having a cigar in his mouth.

It was undergraduates such as these, who established the Upware republic, a sporting club with its headquarters at the Lord Nelson Public House near Wicken fen, rechristened by members as "The Five Miles from anywhere, and No Hurry."

"Here", in the words of James Wentworth Day, the fen historian and naturalist, "young blades ... roistered and drank deep, shot snipe and caught pike, sculled their funnies, fought the bargees for quarts of beer, and drove their high yellow wheeled dog carts behind spanking trotters." [*History of the Fens*. James Wentworth Day. Published in 1954.]

The heydey of the club lasted approximately from 1851 to 1866 covering the period when it is probable that beagles were first brought to Cambridge. A letter written to F.C. Kempson by Dr. Rouse Ball, a mathematical don of Trinity and keen follower of the TFB, mentions this early pack. He writes:

> Going back to a still earlier period, I have been told by old members of the college ... that a pack was kept by Trinity undergraduates in or about 1849, and was dispersed about 1855 or '56.

[Dr. Rouse Ball was the author of a memorable book on string games, a copy of which always used to be found in the guest rooms at Trinity. I have not been able to discover any record of string having been provided.]

H.S. Gladstone, master in 1899, also refers to it in a short history he compiled as a preface to his hunting diary. And its existence is further corroborated by accounts of the activities of one Henry Charles Russell an undergraduate of Trinity about 1858. According to his grandson, who whipped-in to the TFB in 1933, his grandfather used to beagle in the intervals allowed by his other serious activities viz: ferreting, pike fishing, skating, snipe shooting, poaching of various sorts and studying to take orders. Unfortunately there are no other records to substantiate the existence of this early beagle pack.

The first pack of hounds to be kept by undergraduates that is documented, was the drag; and it was for the purpose of drag hunting that the first known pack of beagles was also brought to Cambridge. The earliest mention of drag hunting appears in 1849 in *Sketches of Cantabs* when a typical line is described by a bewildered North American. The participants having assembled, began their day by drinking at a public house. He continues: "At length after nearer forty than ten minutes had been spent at this kind of work, the signal was given to horse ..." Then they all took off at a gallop across country heedless of the destruction they caused. The day ended in a pitch battle between undergraduates and farmers during which:

> ... sticks and stones darkened the air – student and bandit were in one place locked together in deadly combat – in another some horse without a rider was galloping wild and exultant along the road. Blood flowed everywhere like water ...

It was to pursue this sport that in 1862 R.G. Hoare, then an undergraduate at Magdalene introduced a private pack of beagles to Cambridge which he hunted as a foot drag. The five or six couple of hounds were kennelled at Callaby's, the dog fancier, who had a stable and a rat pit in the enclosure known as Fort St. George, by the river on Midsummer Common. Callaby's establishment is immortalised in Charles Stuart Calverley's poem *Hic Vir, Hic Est* [Published 1862]. In it Calverley recalls his undergraduate days of the 1850s:

> Struck at Brown's, the dashing hazard;
> Or (more curious sport than that)
> Dropped, at Callaby's the terrier,
> Down upon the prisoned rat.

Callaby himself is admirably described by F.C. Kempson:

> He wore a top hat, a white spotted blue choker over a Gladstone collar, a short black cutaway coat with side pockets, and tight fitting trousers ... he had very thick leather gloves for handling his rats.

Although R.G. Hoare had originally acquired his beagles with the intention of hunting drag lines, he soon gave in to the irresistable temptation to hunt hares. When he went down from Cambridge an undergraduate called Courtney Tracey, who later became the famous master of Otter Hounds, formed another pack. He drafted hounds from packs in Kent and Cambridgeshire and from the Christchurch Beagles, (the latter were at that time being temporarily disbanded in favour of Harriers). They met at 1.45 p.m. and hunted hares all round Station Road, Histon Observatory, Cherry Hinton and Coton. H.H. Bagnall the first whipper-in took on the mastership the following season, but he could find no successor, and in 1866 this extremely promising "foot drag" was disbanded.

The following year, an assistant tutor of Trinity, William Edward Currey brought over from his home in Ireland a pack of 18 couple of 15 inch hounds. This was the turning point for beagling in Cambridge. W.E. Currey, a graduate of Trinity, was an easy-going Irishman, who brilliantly combined his rôles as tutor and master of hounds. His enthusiasm and sociability attracted undergraduates to the sport of hare hunting, and his leadership so established the pack, that it became a permanent feature of Cambridge life. He hunted all round Cambridge including Waterbeach, Comberton, Fulbourne, Barton and Hardwick, country which is still hunted today. Mr. C.R.G. Hoare, a keen follower, describes how Currey used to hunt hounds:

He used to ride an extraordinary clever cob of about 14.2, a marvel over fen ditches or anything else. Mr. Currey was a good horseman, and I should say a very good harehunter, and I never remember his taking advantage of his field, who were toiling on foot.

When Currey was preoccupied with tutorial matters, his whipper-in C.M. Meysey-Thompson, hunted hounds, becoming the first undergraduate huntsman of the "Foot Beagles". This precedent ensured that when Currey left the University, which he did in 1870, there was sufficient interest amongst undergraduates to carry on running a pack of beagles themselves.

For the next ten years each new master, in succession, bought the pack from his predecessor, and continued to hunt the country established by W.E. Currey. Initially they continued as riding huntsmen and it was not until 1874 when G.H. Longman became master, that they dispensed with the necessity of cobs and took to their feet instead. In 1880 the position of the hunt was strengthened by the brilliant mastership of Rowland Hunt, who extended the country, improved the hounds and increased the following of undergraduates. He had had exactly the same effect upon the Eton College Hunt a few years earlier and such was his reputation that crowds of Old Etonians flocked to subscribe to the Trinity Foot beagles when they heard he was to become master.

However it was not under Roland Hunt's mastership, but at the end of Viscount Milton's, in 1892, that a significant change of policy was made. The custom of the retiring master selling the pack to the incoming one had so far ensured a quarter-century of continuous hunting, but it was a continuity that could be at any moment broken – as it had been in 1866 – and besides it precluded any consistent breeding policy, particularly as masters tended to take their favourite hounds down with them. Viscount Milton handed the pack to his successor, R.S. Hicks, on the understanding that it remained his property only for the duration of his mastership, and he in turn undertook on going down to leave the same number of hounds to the next master in line. From that date the continuation of the pack was secured. In addition to his wise change of policy Viscount Milton also bequeathed a silver horn, which is handed down from master to master as a badge of office.

The reason why the pack was named after Trinity College is uncertain. During W.E. Currey's mastership the pack was referred to simply as the Foot Beagles, but the name of Trinity must always have been associated with them, not only because Currey was a member of that college, but so many other early masters were as well. Perhaps Trinity was also considered the natural college for sportsmen, whether they were members or not. This fact is best illustrated by an answer given by the Hon. George Lambton to a gentleman workwatcher at Newmarket at the turn of the century. On being asked what college he belonged to he replied: "I don't know. Trinity I suppose."

It was during Rowland Hunt's mastership that a livery was adopted. This is ironic for Hunt was a notoriously bad dresser, whose shirt tails, of great length, regularly used to fly out behind him whilst hunting. Until his mastership the only distinguishing feature of a hunt servant's uniform was a Lincoln green cloth cap, and the TFB button. The latter was introduced during V.W. Vickers mastership (1874–7) and consisted of "T.F.B." stamped in black capitals on the silver face. In 1880 a green velvet coat became the uniform of master and whips; and in 1882 the cloth cap was discarded for a hard velvet cap. The first hunt coats were made by Bainbridge in Trinity Street, although in later years members had them made by their respective Cambridge tailors. Geoffrey Dent (who whipped-in from 1912–3) had his made by Barnet Beale in Trinity Street where presumably his white breeches were made too, for by the turn of the century they had become the norm. His beagling boots were made by Flack near the Round Church. The velvet coats turned not only the weather, but thorns as well. They lasted for years: Geoffrey Dent wore his for farming purposes until it became so tattered that it was eventually used for catching peaches in his kitchen garden. In the 1960s the expense of velvet coats led some members to adopt green felt coats instead.

Not long after the master and his whips adopted this distinguished livery, the Beagle Club was formed. This took place on November 9th, 1892 in the rooms of the master, R.S. Hicks. The rules which were drawn up have dictated the activities of the beagle club ever since:

1. That this club be called the Beagle Club.
2. That the Master of the Trinity Foot Beagles shall for the time being be the President.
3. That the Committee shall consist of the master and the three whips of the Trinity Foot Beagles, any two of which and the master shall form a quorum.
4. That the club shall consist of not more than six members.
5. That the club shall dine once a week in one member's rooms.
6. That the member in whose rooms the dinner is held shall have the privilege of inviting one guest.
7. That the club dress be white waistcoat, green velvet coat with lighter green silk facings, and silver hares on each side of the collar.
8. That any former member shall have the privilege of dining with the club.
9. That one black ball in three shall exclude, and that the President shall have a casting vote.

10.   That a general meeting may be called at any time by the President.

Membership of the club cost £2 and there was a £10 annual subscription, paid by each whip. This proved an important source of income for the master and ensured that the pack remained independent of college and university support. Only once has an attempt been made to link the pack to a college financially. This occurred in 1899 during H.S. Gladstone's mastership, when a member proposed that the TFB should join the Amalgamated Athletics Club of Trinity. This would have placed the pack in a position similar to that of the Christchurch at Oxford. Fortunately the motion was not carried. In recent years this decision has served the TFB to advantage as, unlike the Christchurch, it has never been faced with the unexpected collapse of an important source of income from a particular college.

This independence, with its reliance upon neither "county" nor university support, explains the resilience and unique character of the Trinity Foot Beagles. It is reflected in their long tradition of hunting not less than three days every week during the Michaelmas and Lent terms; in their pioneering of September beagling in Northumberland; and in the practically unbroken line of undergraduate masters, who receive the title "Master of Hounds", long before they receive that of Bachelor of Arts or of Master of Foxhounds. Two honours which naturally take second place to that which signifies the most ancient and distinguished art of venery.

CHAPTER TWO

THE COUNTRY

As at present registered, the boundaries of the Trinity Foot Beagles' hunting country follow the limits exercised by the pack since the last century, stretching from Royston in the south to Earith in the north, and from Swaffham Prior in the east to Sandy and Kimbolton in the west. They form no regular pattern, but correspond in size and shape to the territory of the Cambridgeshire Foxhounds, while in addition the Trinity Foot Beagles share the country to the east of Cambridge with the Cambridgeshire Harriers.

To the west the neighbouring pack of beagles is the North Bucks; while to the south and the south east the TFB march with the West Lodge Harehounds and the De Burgh and North Essex Bassets respectively. Since there are no rival packs to the north, the TFB are free to hunt as far afield as the Wash itself if they so desire. But for practical reasons the pack has, in the main, chosen to hunt inside a fifteen mile radius from the centre of Cambridge and within these self-appointed limits three distinct types of country are to be found. F.C. Kempson describes them as follows: first, the plough country, which is "cold, grey and most adhesive ..."; second, the woodlands "fruit gardens that is, orchards of standard trees with pretty dense undergrowth of currant and gooseberry bushes planted between the rows"; and finally the fens, "sheer flat black peaty soil reclaimed from a state of swamp ... the fields are divided by dykes full of water which have to be jumped clean ... the vast open space of the fen is strangely compelling and attractive."

Most masters temper their strong inclination for the fens and try and hunt the entire country equally. In no part of the Cambridgeshire landscape is there any shortage of hares: throughout, the large fields of beet and cabbage provide a magnificent diet for the hare population.

The plough country runs to the south of the line of the Huntington Road to Cambridge's west, and of the Cambridge-Newmarket branch railway to its east. The change in soil between the fens and the plough is quite distinct as Sir Ralph Clarke noted in his hunting diary when writing up a meet at Lode in November 1911. After a good hunt of $2^1/_2$ hours on the same hare Clarke remarks: "Spent some time at the end of the fen near the line this is clay-gault soil not fen, the junction between them was well shown in a fresh-cut drain."

Its clay content makes this ploughland in all probability the heaviest running country in Britain particularly since it is by no means flat; it has strained the hearts of at least two masters W.W. Hicks-Beach (1928–29) and J. Dimsdale (1932–33); and left innumerable followers in a state of near collapse.

In his book *Horn and Hound* H.A. Bryden describes a typical day over the plough during W.H. Whitbread's mastership (1921–23) when the field met at the Wheatsheaf, Harlton, and comprised only eleven men:

> Round Harlton the country is a very sticky clay, and after the frost, snow and thaw it was indescribably heavy; in fact I never hunted on foot under worse conditions. With each stride, one raised on either foot two or three pounds weight of clay. We found a hare quickly and followed her as best we could; there was no scent and she soon ran us out of that necessity. We found again before long, and after surmounting a low hill twice and hunting slowly for forty minutes we were again defeated. Cold showers kept beating up to add to our difficulties ... Found again and once more, after another forty minutes hunt, during which Whitbread, his whips, and his good little pack worked very hard, we were again run clean out of scent and were all fairly beat by the desperately heavy going. This was without exception the worst day for getting over a country that I ever encountered ... I was stiff for some days after this bout of foot-slogging over seas of the stickiest and most holding plough I can remember in a long experience.

The most famous area of plough is that around Grantchester and Trumpington, over which the Pemberton family have acted as generous hosts to the TFB for many years, and not least in giving them a joint meet with the drag at Trumpington Hall, before the Hunt Ball every Michaelmas term. The highly sensitive apparatus of the University's Department of Astronomy is encompassed by this area and it, along with its predecessor on the Madingley Road, has been continually threatened by the Trinity Foot Beagles. In 1951 Rex Hancock and his hounds, on a screaming scent, hunted right across the present site, just as the astronomers thought they had detected a war on Mars. This stretch of country between Grantchester and Barton is currently the vast earthworks of Cambridge's western by-pass, a presence which causes much sinking of heart to beaglers and radio astronomers alike.

The ploughland to the south and southwest of Cambridge is watered by the River Cam, its branches and tributaries – the Granta, the Rhee and the Bourn brook – dividing the land around Grantchester, Trumpington, Haslingfield and Hauxton into a series of natural draws. Occasionally a river has had to be swum by the hunt staff, but this is not such a regular occurrence as it is among

Typical drawing taken from the *Beagle Club Dinner Books*. It depicts Victor Seely (*raising cap at left*), deputy master to Gilbert Dunning, and Dewar Harrison (*right*), a whipper-in, crossing the Cam in a canoe at Grantchester in 1920.

the network of slow rivers and drains of the fens. During H.S. Gladstone's mastership in 1899, he and his whips were saved a wetting when hounds killed their hare in mid-stream. The hunt had met at Hauxton mill over land owned by the Hurrells of Newton Hall, a family who from early times offered the pack a welcome. And while talking of good friends of the TFB in the Upper Cam valley, in recent years the squire of Whittlesford, Mr. Kim Tickell has proved a great ally by offering his hostelry, the Tickell Arms as the venue for the opening meet. This launches the season with suitable brio at the beginning of each Michaelmas term.

To the west of Cambridge, and a little further out, but still in clay country, the villages of Lolworth and Boxworth provide some excellent meets, and in 1957 for the first time, one was arranged at the newly-named Trinity Foot public house at Swavesey Corner. It is of no coincidence that the company which owned the property had an ex-master of the TFB, W.H. Whitbread, as its Managing Director. No doubt it was he who chose the subject for the inn sign, namely Rowland Hunt running with his hounds, but minus his famous shirt tails flapping in the breeze. The master of the time C.H.A. Bott, boldly requested a subscription from the company. Back came the dignified reply from the Board:

> We are pleased to donate the sum of £10 towards the TFB. This is not necessarily an annual subscription but will be considered each year.

The approximate boundary of the plough country is the stretch of the old Ermine Street between Godmanchester and Royston. This has been hunted since before the First World War, when Ralph Clarke drove by coach as far as Longstowe Hall, where his fast pack encountered enormous numbers of hares on "very sticky country". The TFB still meet at Longstowe every Lent term by courtesy of Mr. and Mrs. Bevan, whose delicious teas have helped make this one of the most popular meets of the season.

While these parts of the Cambridgeshire landscape remain to a large extent unchanged, there is a stretch of country, which has been permanently spoilt. This is the area now covered by the outskirts of Cambridge. Meets used for example to be held in Girton Village, on Trinity Backs and at Barnwell, Chesterton Cross Roads and Fen Ditton. The last three were no longer hunted by the 1930s. And it is perhaps fortunate that a few years later the meet at Girton village was abandoned due to development, because it frequently resulted in complaints being registered by the Principal of the college. The most spectacular cause for complaint occurred in 1931 during W.J. Stirling's mastership. His hounds put up a hare in a field of rough grass near the

Robert Rous, master in 1974, photographed after a meet at Longstowe Hall.

A meet at the Red Lion, Grantchester. John Buxton (*centre*) is master. He is one of many of his family to have served with the TFB. On Buxton's right, in uniform, is Rex Hancock who succeeded as master in 1951.

Moving off from Trinity Backs in the spring of 1930. (*From left to right*) Norman Hart, Bob Hoare (*in front*), Peter Paget, master, and John Ridell (*at back*).

Hounds working out a line after a meet at Longstowe Hall in 1974.

Huntington Road and hunted her straight into the grounds of Girton College. To complicate matters the pack was augmented by the entire complement of drag hounds, who joined in on their way home from a meet. This very promising hunt ended when the hare ran straight into the coal house where it was duly despatched. Later it is uncertain whether the Principal's subsequent complaints were on the grounds of compassion for the hare or concern for the virtue of her young ladies. No longer are masters free to hunt the hare in the forty leafy acres of Girton grounds, but there is compensation in the number of Girtonians who now follow the hunt, although their motives cannot always be attributed to a love of venery.

Trinity Backs remained a regular meet until 1955 when Simon Cresswell held the last one there with two mounted whips in attendance. The custom of meeting in the precincts of Trinity was temporarily revived in 1959 by Simon Scrope, who met at Trinity Great Gate and moved off across the Backs, miraculously avoiding a drag which some wit had laid across Great Court to the Master's lodge. It had been traditional for the group photograph of the Field and pack to be taken on Trinity Backs and many a hunting correspondent has begun his report: "Having faced the camera on the Backs we moved off in the direction of Coton Thorns."

The only possible draw was towards Coton and over the rifle range at the back of the University rugby ground. Only once (when H.C. Howard was master in 1871) did the pack run back into Cambridge, F.C. Kempson recorded the adventure as follows:

> After a meet on the Backs they had a good hunt in the direction of Coton, over Trinity cricket ground, through Burrell's field, and over Trinity Garden to Clare College Bridge. When they got to the bridge there was the hare in the water and somehow she scrambled up the ivy and ran into the court. By this time Harry Howard was off his horse and running down the avenue, blowing his horn to get his hounds onto the line. He laid them on, on the grass in the courtyard. As he was doing so the Master Dr. Atkinson, came out, in his tall hat and frock coat. He was in a blue rage:
>
> "Such an outrage has never been committed in the history of the University."
>
> Harry couldn't see it, and wasn't for drawing off the hounds. But the Master got more and more angry, and managed to turn them out, beagles and all ... [Dr. Atkinson was elected to the Mastership in 1856 and was incumbent until 1915. His predecessor had been elected in 1815, their combined residence spanned a century, which is surely a record.]

C.H.A. Goodwin, a whipper-in, in 1976. Ankle deep in typical plough country at Barrington.

If the plough country is the heaviest ground over which the Trinity Foot hunt, then the woodland country is the most frustrating. It intersperses both the plough and the fen country, with a preponderance around Cottenham, Histon and Hardwick, the principal centres of fruit farming in Cambridge. This industry took off in the county after 1873, when the Chivers family established their fruit bottling and jam factory close to the station at Histon. Within twenty years over 3000 acres of land in the vicinity of Histon alone had been put down to orchard.

The difficulties of hunting this ground are described by Charlie Barclay in his diary after a day in 1939 when he was whipping-in from Twenty Pence Bridge. The field enjoyed a five-mile point running from the orchard at the back of the Jolly Waterman up to the racecourse and back again to the orchard. That night he wrote it up:

> A good hunt of about 6$^1/_2$ miles over an abominable line of country. These orchards are ghastly things to hunt through as one cannot see anything ...

The woodland country also means a good deal of drudgery for those whipping-in as Michael Dill wrote in his diary of a meet at Comberton the following year:

> We put up a hare on the Comberton and Toft side and I had to guard Chivers' orchards and stop hounds if she went in there ... I ran up and down the hedge in front of Mr. Chivers' strawberries all day, however she foxed me by going round and back over the strawberries. We were able to get hounds back on ... and after a scramble killed her in a little pond.

They deserved their reward, after a hunt of 1 hour and 35 minutes.

The Trinity Foot have always been most closely associated with the fen country. They have had the good fortune to attract strong local support from this area, and have made the fen town of Cottenham the centre of their social and sporting activities. Their hunting has been confined to the fenlands South of the River Nene and in particular to a stretch of the South Level between the Old Bedford river and the highland around Cambridge. These fens were drained considerably later than the alluvial levels of South Lincolnshire. As late as 1609 it was said of James I:

> For the honour of his Kingdom, He would no longer suffer these countries to be abandoned to the will of the waters, nor let them lie waste and unprofitable.

Elaborate and ruinously expensive schemes were put in motion, which were so impeded by the intrigues at Court, Parliamentary rebellion and natural disasters, that no real progress was made until thirty years later when William, Earl of Bedford, created the Three Levels in 1649. The South Level, over which the TFB hunt most regularly, is drained principally by the Old and New Bedford Rivers and by the old West River. The latter follows the original course of the Ouse; it is canalised and its tall banks and the vivid green of the "washes" within are a dominant landmark winding through the best fenland hunting country of the TFB.

Every point on its course has its historic associations. It enters the fens at Over, where the TFB have met since the days when they travelled there by coach and put up at the inn by the ferry, the Pike and Eel; it borders the Upper Delphs at Earith the man-made washland where generations of beaglers have skated and flighted duck as well as hunted. Six miles north of Cottenham it divides the country, and that ground between the town and the river offers some of the most famous draws of the TFB. These include Smithey Fen (pronounced by the locals Smithafen), Hensals Fen at the back of Rampton and Twenty Pence Bridge. North of the river lies some of the remotest fenland, the capital of which is the village of Aldreth. This is reputed to be the scene of the first fen meet ever arranged by W.E. Currey for his Foot Beagles and it remains to this day an excellent choice. The River Great Ouse leaves the territory of the TFB and joins the River Cam at Streatham Mere; this is country which has been hunted since 1886 when A.F. Pease enjoyed a $2^1/$ hour run there after a fox. To the east of the River Cam, which runs north from Cambridge to meet the Ouse, lie the fen meets on the boundary with the chalk highlands. These take place near the villages of Burwell, the Swaffham Prior and Bulbeck and Stow-cum-Quy.

Wherever they are encountered both rivers present formidable barriers to masters and whips who are forced on occasions to swim after their less inhibited pack. There are some highly graphic passages in hunting diaries relating to swims in the fens, including having to break the ice before doing so or merely taking the plunge in a snow storm. On one occasion in 1932 from a meet at Twenty Pence Bridge the hunt staff had to swim the Old West no less than twice in each direction. Masters soon learnt to throw their horn and whip over with their hearts, and to hold their velvet coats above their heads whilst taking the plunge. Before they do so they have often been treated to the sight of hounds swimming the river in full cry, as scent carries on stagnant water.

The one area of the country that has been spoilt by modern development is along the Cambridge-Ely road. Up until the Second World War three of the best meets were held in this area: at the Slap Up at Waterbeach, the Traveller's Rest at Chittering and at Denny Abbey. The latter was of interest not only because it provided an excellent draw over North Fen but also because the transept of the old Abbey church was adapted in the 17th-century to become the farm house while a barn is reputed to be the old refectory. The expansion of Waterbeach aerodrome has ruined most of this country for hunting, and now only one meet remains at Milton.

Other changes have been more gradual: it was not until 1929 that the soft drove road between Cottenham and Twenty Pence Bridge was macadamed, and well into this century it was possible to detect dialects peculiar to remote fen villages. The appearance and demography of the fens have greatly altered as a result of changes in the traditional methods of farming. Ralph Norman, who reigns as King of Cottenham, and who has supported the beagles since he was a boy remembers the years before and immediately after the First World War when two hundred to three hundred men would daily go down to work on Smithey and Setchel Fens. Corroboration of this is found in Ralph Clarke's diary which abounds with comments referring to agricultural workers who were useful to the whips for the information they could give as to the whereabouts of the hunted hare. In the 1920s and 1930s these workers were to leave Cottenham in such large numbers, that the population of the town fell by three thousand. Before the First World War horses were in use everywhere, and the harvest was carted into Cottenham and stored in the barns at the back of the houses. There was also a great deal more stock on the land, for Cottenham had been traditionally a great dairy country, renowned for its cheese. Smithey Fen was all grass and hedgerows and Ralph Clarke encountered stretches of grass at Bottisham, Earith and Swaffham Prior. Today no trace of this era remains: the stables are empty; the turf is under plough; and the secret of Cottenham cheese is lost for ever. [The best double Cottenham cheese was sold by Flack and Judge, grocer's opposite Emmanuel, as late as 1939. Ralph Norman presented the last known cheese press, found in his cellar, to the Cambridge Folk Museum.] One reason for the rapid change from dairy to arable farming in the 1920s was the development of sugar beet as a profitable crop. The process was accelerated by the arrival of technology in the form of steam ploughs and giro tillers. The latter were hated by beaglers, not only did they erase all scent, but turned the springy peat topsoil into quicksand, making running impossible. J.J. Mann after a day at Waterbeach wrote angrily in his diary: "Scent completely failed on a bl**dy bit of giro tilled land."

Many non-Cambridge beaglers would not agree with F.C. Kempson's remark that the fens are a beaglers paradise, but they still have a great many advantages over other countries. It is cold scenting country and, for the young huntsman learning his craft, it provides ample time for him to watch hounds work out a line. It is not such a good country for followers, who are rarely inspired to run any great distance, but many find that the immense skies, the blood-red sunsets, the black earth and the piercing spire, form a remote and compelling landscape.

The three categories of country described by F.C. Kempson remain valid today, but to present an exact picture a fourth must also be added. It is that of invitation meets, which have become a feature of the card since the early 50s.

It was J.J. Buxton (master 1950–51) who first made full use of plentiful supplies of petrol after the war to accept invitations to meet beyond the traditional boundaries, many of which are still extended to the pack today. The two longest standing invitations are to meet at Brent Pelham and Bentfieldbury in Essex. By offering hospitality to the TFB at Brent Pelham, the Barclay family showed their typical generosity to the pack which has been evident throughout its history. A number of excellent days have resulted from this meet, although hares are notoriously difficult to find. The meet at Bentfieldbury provides the TFB with some much needed grassland. This meet was offered to John Buxton by Mr. Chester, who whilst up at Cambridge in 1914 and 1919 had been a keen supporter of the TFB. In 1969 another invitation meet was added to the list by Mr. Webb of Streetely Hall, West Wickham. Mr. Webb is in his 70s and still at the time of writing hunts three days a week with the Cambridgeshire and acts as host to them as well as to the local Harriers, Drag, Bassets and now Beagles. A number of exceptional days have been enjoyed from Streetely Hall, including one in 1975 when Ted Foster killed his hare on the steps of the police station in Horseheath High Street. Another meet offered in the following year was at Great Bradley Hall by Mr. and Mrs. Ryder; this resulted in Stepham Lambert's most memorable day's hunting. He killed one and a half brace after three good hunts, without the help of any of his whips who were lost in a dark wood.

One exchange meet is occasionally arranged with the Pipewell Beagles in Leicestershire. A former master of theirs, Frank Goddard-Jackson, had previously been master of the TFB. Undoubtedly the TFB do best out of the deal, not only in having fine grass country to hunt over, but also afterwards in being regaled with a magnificent tea at which singing plays an integral part of the entertainment. It is then that the Cambridge contingent has a chance to air its voice with the Trinity Foot Song. In return the Pipewell are offered a meet at Haslingfield, where there are plenty of hares, but also acres of taxing plough. The arrival of Diana Bevin, daughter of the Master of the Westerby Bassets, at Girton College in 1975, proved a most fortunate event for beaglers. It led to a joint meet being arranged between the two packs, with basset hunting in the morning and beagling in the afternoon. Hounds met at the Bath Hotel, Scearsby, Leicester and the result was a memorable day. This has now become an annual event, and it is a high point for Cambridge beaglers. The

Westerby Bassets have an even more historic connection with Cambridge. They were founded by Christopher and Godfrey Heseltine in 1889, both of whom were Cambridge undergraduates. During term time they kennelled them at Comberton and enjoyed many excellent days hunting in that area.

Although the core of the TFB country has remained intact a variety has been injected into the season by the addition of the invitation meets. This makes up for the staleness which can occur if the masters have to stick rigidly within their country. Stephen Lambert the most experienced and gifted master of recent years rightly pointed out that it was very difficult to become inspired by the greater part of the TFB's native country, even though it gave one plenty of scope and a good amount of hares. Now a balance has been achieved and the huntsman can enjoy fen, clay, woodland and grass land in the knowledge that he has a wide choice of each.

During the summer, the master and his secretary visit every relevant farmer around Cambridge to seek permission to hunt over his land in the coming season. An invaluable aid in this process is *The Farmers' Book*. This was first compiled by H.G. Carr-Ellison in 1895. In it every meet is given a separate entry, under which the names and addresses of landowners are listed. Successive masters have then added information relating to the temperament of each and the extent of their sympathy towards the TFB. Although the entries have been constantly revised ever since they were first written the type of information the book provides is essentially the same. The book itself received a certain celebrity in 1937 when the hunting correspondent of *The Times* devoted his entire column to its contents, under the headline "The Beagling Tripos."

As *The Farmers' Book* fills up with information, so a new volume is procured. The present volume was compiled by Martin Adam in March 1967. His entries begin by recommending a set rotation of meets, to take into account the requirements of both the Cambridgeshire Foxhounds and the Cambridgeshire Harriers, thus ensuring that none of the three packs clash. In consequence the TFB now meet three days a week; on Tuesdays, Thursdays and Saturdays. On a Tuesday the meet usually takes place in the fens; on a Thursday in the upland country south-west of Cambridge or else by invitation; and on a Saturday within bicycling distance. Of course they frequently enjoy bye-days, and convenient venues are noted in the book.

Since within the TFB's territory there are so many small-holders, particularly in the fens, the number of people who have to be visited is daunting. The prospect of such visits is often made worse if the master should read the comments made by his predecessors about particular individuals, for example:

This man is going mad, he gave me a long sermon on seeking the Kingdom of God, but beaglewise he is quite all right.

To anyone comparing the current book with its predecessors it becomes apparent that certain characteristics such as "if well buttered up A1 chap, nearly always tight in the market", are invariably carried over from father to son. Understandably it is with a sense of relief that the master reads the entry under Quy:

> Fen is commonland no-one to notify except the ghost of William Ison, who according to a memorial was struck by lightning on this spot in August 1854.

Nevertheless rarely if ever do masters encounter serious hostility, a fact which testifies to the generosity of the farming community that surrounds Cambridge and to the good reputation of the pack which has been built up over the years. This began during the mastership of Rowland Hunt (1880–1882), whose tact and friendliness towards farmers resulted in many new meets for the fledgling pack. He was often to be seen in the Corn Exchange, and kept open house in his rooms on market day. His high standards have been maintained and they are enshrined in the "Fifteen points concerning farmers", which appear in *The Farmers' Book*. They form a code of practice founded upon a mixture of commonsense and wisdom, which recommends modesty, courtesy and tolerance towards all those who extend hospitality towards the TFB.

Such is the keenness of Trinity Beaglers that they have always been prepared to travel considerable distances to hunt. In the last century they divided their activities in the field into walking meets, driving meets (within six miles) and other meets (by train), and the earliest edition of *The Farmers' Book* records the distance to each meet as well as convenient inns in which to put up for the night. When it was a driving meet hounds were conveyed in a horse-drawn beagle cart, purposely constructed to Rowland Hunt's specifications in 1880. It replaced a pig cart, and looked like a cross between a hearse and a baker's van; in 1900 when it fell apart from old age, an identical vehicle was constructed which remained in use until 1914.

The driver of this contraption was Mr. Free of Madingly Road who had the contract for taking the hounds to any meet for 10s. unless it was particularly close to Cambridge in which case the emolument was 8s. 6d. It was said that people used to doff their hats to Free as he drove by, for he wore a long black coat and an ancient billycock hat, and this along with his sidewhiskers and fiery nose, led people to imagine that he must be a mute driving a hearse. His old bay horse was very slow and the undergraduates always gave him a good start following on later in brakes drawn by a pair of horses.

The beagle brake had been instituted by H.S. Gladstone in 1899 and at least one would set off from the Pitt Club steps every hunting day. Both brakes and horses were supplied by Hopkins, whose yard was opposite the Fitzwilliam Museum. Subscribers to the brake paid 30s. a term and were conveyed free to all meets on condition that they filled in their names in advance on the list stuck up in Hopkins's yard. Hopkins also provided horses for the rowing coaches and the Cambridge University O.T.C. Cavalry Squadron, so his hirelings were used to any amount of work.

Ralph Clarke's diary shows that the beagle brake was in continual use throughout the season of 1913 when members travelled to Longstowe, Comberton, Longstanton and Swavesey in it. To arrive at the latter it was necessary to load both beagle cart and brake onto the ferry at Overcourt. It was only the outbreak of war in the following year that brought about the demise of the beagle brake, at about the same time that horse trams, a familiar feature of Kings Parade, were also discontinued. Meanwhile the development of the safety bicycle, in the 1890's, and of that great aid to cycling comfort, the pneumatic tyre, eliminated the necessity of walking to meets. And bicycling remained an accepted form of transport to meets until the motorcar became generally available to undergraduates in the 1950's. Once the First World War had come to an end and serious beagling could be resumed the problem of transport was temporarily overcome by the Deputy Master, Victor Seely, who provided a huge Napier Shooting wagon, originally designed to transport Edwardian shots from covert to covert, which carried as many as twenty beaglers at a time to "driving" meets. Unfortunately when Seely left his Napier left with him, and it was replaced by a hired motorbus, which collected beaglers from the steps of the Pitt Club. This was arranged by Marshall the Pitt Club steward, who soon saw the possibilities of providing a similar kind of service, but with different routes, to members of the general public. As a result he left club service to set up a garage a few yards further down Jesus Lane which flourishes to this day.

Once old Free and his cart had been laid up, the hounds were conveyed to the meet in a trailer towed by the master's car. The latter was very old and of an unreliable nature and on one occasion J.J. Dimsdale saw the trailer full of hounds part from his car and career away down Cottenham High Street.

Apart from the early years of the Second World War, which will be described in a later chapter when the master reverted to horse drawn transport, the motor car has become the Trinity Foot's staple means of transport. Thus a new dimension has been added to the Trinity Beagler's gift for speed, enabling him not only to race on nimble foot after the hunted hare, but also to career across the breadth of his hunting country in cars of every shape and age.

CHAPTER THREE

COTTENHAM

Of all church towers in the fens, that of Cottenham, crowned with fanciful 17th-century battlements and pinnacles, is surely the most singular. It stands at the far end of the High Street, on the perimeter of the fen, and dominates the surrounding landscape. The town is long and narrow consisting of substantial yellow-brick farmhouses backed with large barns and yards. It would be hard to compare Cottenham to any other English town for it most closely resembles a Spanish pueblo, with its inhabitants going out into the surrounding flat countryside to work. Cottenham has never come under the influence of a single landowner; the largest surviving house is the Queen Anne rectory; and the community is led by prosperous farmers.

The TFB have always been warmly welcomed in the town, indeed to such an extent that it has become their second home. This is largely thanks to the influence of a few staunch Cottenham supporters, who took it upon themselves to act as ambassadors between the undergraduate and agricultural community. In turn the TFB act as hosts to the inhabitants of Cottenham at their point-to-point held on the outskirts of the town. This is an event of great antiquity, which has helped form Cottenham's reputation as the sporting as well as the social centre of the TFB.

Let us pay tribute to some of our Cottenham friends. "Duke" Ivatt was the first ambassador for the TFB in Cottenham. His father farmed at Rampton, where during the mastership of Rowland Hunt, he was often host to the beagles. Duke himself owned the farm at Twenty Pence Bridge (now farmed by Richard Graves, who will be encountered again as a hero of the annual cricket match), but this land he let to a tenant. His main pre-occupation was shooting, and he had the sporting rights all over the fens around Cottenham. He was considered one of the best shots in the county and when he was in his prime in the 1920s he was reckoned to average about 1000 partridges to his gun every year. Perhaps his greatest service to the Trinity Foot Beagles was in preserving the hare population of the countryside around Cambridge from the random depredations of local men and their lurchers, by forbidding any coursing across land to which he had rights. In addition he opened up new country for the beagles. He introduced the pack to the fen behind Rampton in

1913; and he revived the meet at Streatham in 1939, which had lapsed for many years. C.G.E. Barclay whipping-in on the day in question, remarked in his diary:

> A new meet arranged by Mr. Ivatt and an excellent one too. There appear to be just the right amount of hares in this piece of country.

Over the years, Duke's activities have become part of folklore. He was famous for being able to catch a hare in its form, and could, at a distance, readily tell a jack from a doe. He also had a splendid recipe for lapses of memory, consisting of hard boiled eggs and watercress from fen ditches. The last reference to Duke appears in Michael Dill's diary, on March 11th 1940, at a meet at Rampton:

> J (Julian Holland-Hibbert) drew park first and Mr. Ivatt (looking very old and frail but in good fettle) put up a hare. She took us for a flying 35 minutes round the outskirts of Rampton.

Duke outlived the last war and died in Cottenham in 1948.

His successor, Billy Savidge, lived in Denmark Road a little out of the town, and farmed in a small way on the fens. He took over those duties that Duke Ivatt had previously performed, and was noted for his dry humour. One day Billy was down on Smithey Fen when, close by, the pack put up a hare. After a time he went to fetch his bicycle and rode over towards the racecourse to milk his cow, which he kept in an adjoining field. Soon he heard the noise of hounds coming his way and suddenly they burst through a hedge and killed their hare at his feet. Eventually the master who had last seen Billy on Smithey Fen came running up and asked him in some amazement how he had managed to be in at the kill. Billy, adding bi-location to his other powers enquired in turn: "Didn't you see me running in front of you."

Billy Savidge died in 1965 and since then Ralph Norman has undertaken the responsibility of advising and helping the TFB. It was a role for which he must surely have been preparing himself since birth. He was born in Cottenham and first remembers seeing the four-wheeled equipages, laden with green-clad beaglers, bowling down the High Street in 1912 when he was aged ten. His imagination fired, he therefore took every opportunity to follow the hunt. Often when grilled by his father on the progress of the day's work he had to admit that the beagles had been down on the fen that day and no work had been done at all. On one occasion when he was out hedging on Smithey Fen (he and his father farmed at Engine Drove) W.J. Stirling and his pack ran past in furious pursuit and Ralph, forgetting that he was still carrying his

Members of the Cambridge University Whip Club photographed at the varsity point-to-point meeting in March 1938. (*From left to right*) Mark Mainwaring, Michael Dill, Father A.N. Gilbey, A.J. Craig-Harvey, J. Tinsley, Neville Usher, unidentified, Jimmy Bowen and C.G.E. Barclay. Both Dill and Barclay became masters of the TFB.

whetstone joined in the chase and was indeed, first at the kill. Although he is no longer able to maintain his former turn of speed, his enthusiasm remains undimmed, and the favours he renders to the Trinity Foot are legion. Every master who has ever known him remembers his friendship and his kindness to the TFB with deep gratitude and affection.

Let us turn from Cottenham personalities to Cottenham institutions. Part of the town's attraction for the beaglers has been its pubs. Two in particular stand out as historic landmarks and indeed are part of history now, having in the last few years closed their doors to fen folk and thirsty beaglers alike. They were the Jolly Waterman, which stood half a mile outside the town, where the drove goes off into Smithey Fen; and the Three Horse Shoes, at the church end of the High Street. It was here that some of the most sumptuous and riotous beagling teas took place, teas that were usually not undeserved as a description of a hunt from Twenty Pence Bridge under J.J. Mann's mastership will demonstrate:

> A hare turned and piercing a strong line of defence entered the kale never to come forth again. A village concert equipped with fog horns, nightingales and sirens would not have produced more beautiful music than that which brought hounds from covert on this occasion. They drew afresh, but during this operation a veritable monsoon crashed upon us. Dim figures were seen groping about searching for a hare, but none could be found. The Master blew hounds home and the field made for the Jolly Waterman with all possible speed.

The landlord of this hospitable establishment was Edgar Gifford. The isolation of his pub meant that he was a law unto himself especially when it came to the provision of beagle teas. Edgar's wife Ethel could be relied on for anything from rook pie to hot rum and milk, with the milk coming straight from the cow, which stood to be milked in the tap room. Before the beaglers set to to gorge themselves Ethel would take care of any clothes which had taken a soaking – as was often the case – and put them to dry in front of a roaring fire.

After such a tea at the Jolly Waterman it was a favourite sport for beaglers to take on the locals to a race from lamp-post to lamp-post down Cottenham High Street. One farmer, carrying another on his back, would run fifty yard intervals, against a beagler similarly handicapped who would run one hundred yards. Champions at this sport were Billy and Horace Savidge and Harry Ivatt. Horace Savidge was brother of Ted Savidge, but no relation to Billy (generations of inter-marriage has resulted in whole tribes of fen folk all bearing the same name, but claiming no kinship whatever); Harry Ivatt was son of Duke.

The other haven for tired and hungry beaglers was the Three Horse Shoes run by the famous "Mother" Palmer. Her spreads were not so much teas as feasts. She would regularly order £7 worth of meat from Rose's in Petty Cury. Then followed (for Mrs. Palmer is Scottish) huge mounds of griddle scones and bread and butter.

From this it will have become apparent that Trinity Foot Beaglers do not display normal appetites at tea time. This caused the Rev. F.C. Kempson great concern when he entertained them at his vicarage at Manea:

> I wonder what they say of me. I only gave them sandwiches, bread and cheese, cake, beer and whisky stand-up fashion before hunting, and the things normal people have at tea time viz tea, bread, butter, diverse cakes, and little buns and jam. No hot sausages, port wine or cigars and certainly no bubbly wine.

If the TFB were dissatisfied with the generosity of this churchman, they were certainly never disappointed with the teas of Canon Maurice, Rector of Cottenham from 1937–64. Once every season he would dispense lavish hospitality after hunting, often bedding down the hounds in his stable for the duration. The Canon's wife was the genius behind these famous teas: she came from Northumberland, a county well used to nurturing Trinity Foot beaglers. But whatever marvels Mrs. Maurice may have produced, they can scarcely have rivalled an original and favourite treat which Colonel Francis used to give the Trinity Foot at Quy Hall: poached eggs on home made crumpets.

The sense of well being consequent on such occasions colours the accounts of many days hunting. Here is a typical extract from Michael Dill's diary describing a return journey in his trap after a day at Twenty Pence Bridge:

> We had tea at Gifford's and a drink afterwards at the Three Horse Shoes with Horace, and then back with candles burning in the lamps and a pleasant jig-jog.

But beagling and post-beagling conviviality are not the only bonds between the Trinity Foot and the men of Cottenham. There are other sporting engagements. Racing has been mentioned and, in addition, every year the TFB challenge the Cottenham farmers, or "Fen Tigers" to a cricket match. This was instituted in the 1930s and soon found its rightful place in the calendar, so that nowadays during May week, when undergraduates are feeling at their most hung-over, they have to face amongst other ordeals the terrifying bowling of the one-armed Richard Graves, not to mention the subtle deliveries of Reg and Cyril Savidge (no relation to any other Savidges mentioned already), and Bob Norman (no relation to Ralph). The match is umpired by Colonel Cann who now lives in the rectory. With strict fairness he endeavours to make a different team win each year. [Cricket had been a summer sport much favoured by the beaglers of the 1890s, when H.S. Gladstone and a number of his fellow sportsmen played in a team called the Nihilists.]

One convivial fixture had, regrettably, to give way in the 1930s for a couple of sporting ones. This was the annual dinner, which the Trinity Foot used to give for the farmers jointly with the Harriers. In March 1914 Ralph Clarke rather timidly recorded:

> ... the dinner was a great success. The university fellows were much more excited than the farmers and I thought at one time things would go wrong, but Ivatt told me it was the best dinner for 10 years.

The darts match and the sweepstake are two more recent forms of recreation between the beaglers and the farmers, and somehow the latter usually contrived to win both. The sweepstake takes place in the Hop Bind, a pub again situated in Cottenham High Street, which only became popular with the TFB in the mid-1960s. Here Horace Savidge's brother Ted held court until he died in 1976. Ted was a redoubtable farmer from Rampton, whose dearest delight, on every possible occasion, was to trap the unwary undergraduates into huge insobriety with gentle doses of the Hop Bind's barley wine.

But inevitably the crown of the Cottenham social and sporting calendar is the point-to-point. This is one of the few occasions when a master can express his gratitude in a tangible way to the farmers, who have given the hunt so much help throughout the season. He will distribute free passes among them and entertain them in the Master's tent. Up to 1970 a second meeting was held in May. This, however, was not a permanent Cottenham fixture as it was on occasions held at Marks Tey in Essex. The tradition of holding two point-to-points a season began in the 19th-century when they took place in March and November. But it was the March meeting which was always the smarter of the two and became thought of as the Varsity meeting.

Racing was one of the oldest and most popular diversions among sporting undergraduates. The earliest known course was "The Valley" in Fulbourne, which must be the hollow between Fulbourne windmill and Lord Godolphin's estate on the Gogs. This disappeared under the plough at the time of the Crimean War because of the national need for corn. For a short period the racing fraternity moved to St. Ives, where Hoole, Master of the Drag, broke his neck riding for "The Whip" in 1878. It was not this ill-omen, but the consideration of distance, which in the 1880s caused the course on Mason's Pastures, off Denmark Road in Cottenham parish to be established. An account in *Fores Notes and Sketches* (Volume V, published 1891-2) describes a typical meeting based on that of 1884. The author describes the course, which has changed little to this day:

> The line of trees and big blackthorn hedges that marks the position of the Cottenham course is now in sight; and turning from the main road to the right, up a little gluey lane, we enter the field gate, and go bumping across ridge and furrow to the further side of the course. Here is the line of vehicles taking their stand by the side of the straight finish, and opposite the winning post, the roped-in saddling paddock, and weighing tent, with the historical line of fir trees as a background. The Cottenham course is no cocktail affair or make believe it is as good a course of hunter fences as you could find anywhere in England, and they must either be jumped or let alone.

Undergraduate steeplechasing and drag hunting have always been very closely connected, indeed the early drag hunts tend to be reported in terms more appropriate to a race than to a drag. And it can be fairly safely assumed that the Drag Hounds were responsible for organising the very early point-to-points. Some time towards the end of the 19th-century the Cambridge University United Hunts Club was founded. It was flourishing by 1899, if the frequency of references to it in H.S. Gladstone's hunting diary is anything to go by. The rules stipulated that members must be elected from the ranks of the Drag and of the TFB and its raison d'être was and remains, the organisation of point-to-points. In the 19th-century one of the greatest difficulties besetting the organisers was to estimate the amount of compensation that should be paid to those small holders over whose land the races were run. It was particularly unfortunate that the most cantankerous owner, Mr. Cash, a cook at St. John's, also happened to own three quarters of the pastures. After the 1890 meeting, Mr. Cash and his neighbours between them were not to be fobbed off with less than 12 dozen bottles of whisky. But more recently all the land comprising the course has been under the single ownership of the Cambridgeshire Harriers; under this sensible arrangement, the Hunt Club now pay them an annual rent.

The 19th-century organisers employed the town crier of Cottenham to collect the gatemoney and hired two dozen Cambridge policemen (at 12s. a dozen) to keep law and order. One striking feature of the earlier meetings was the large number of mounted spectators who rather than adopt a single viewpoint, preferred to gallop from point to point to view the progress of the race. This lent further confusion to a scene already crowded with coaches and traps, top-heavy with undergraduates and their elaborate luncheon hampers. At the end of such a meeting these vehicles which had come leisurely out from Cambridge were raced pell-mell back, and there the festivities continued afresh, supervised no doubt by the same two dozen policemen, who were retained for the duration of the day. H.S. Gladstone described the end to a typical "varsity" meeting in his hunting diary of 1899:

> Thursday November 25th saw us all at Cottenham. No less than three coaches turned up, and it was an A1 meeting. The Baron (Rothschild) did well and won several races. Perhaps the most enjoyable part of the day was the drive back in our coach to Cambridge: "Cat" handled the ribbons perfectly marvellously and we did the 7 miles in 31 minutes, three minutes more than it took us last year. We had numerous carts and carriages to pass and he only crashed into one. I never touched a winner all day. In the evening I attended the Althanaeum T, which broke up the bannisters and went about belabouring everything with them. We invaded the Hoop and Magdalene and tried to wreck both, the police followed us, but we got home all right, even unprogged.

The earliest race meetings sported a varied card. The November event consisted of three steeplechases, two races over hurdles, two on the flat, and at the end of the day a hurdle and a flat race apiece for ponies under 14.2 hands. In 1898 the master of the drag discontinued the last two events as "they in no way added to the dignity and entertainment of the meeting." At the March meeting the most famous event which took place was the Whip Race. The whip had been presented in 1861 by N. de Rothschild and the Hon. H.W. Fitzwilliam:

> To be run for annually over a course of fair hunting country, calculated to bring out the best in a well schooled hunter and an intelligent rider with a good eye for the country.

The contestants had both to be members of the university and also to have hunted with the Drag. W.H. Whitbread is so far the only master of the TFB to have won the whip; he did so on the same occasion on which he also won the Athenaeum Cup, the second most sought after prize of the "Varsity Meeting". In later years he went on to ride twice in the Grand National, so presumably his experience on Mason's Pastures stood him in good stead. Since 1953 the whip has been awarded to the first Cambridge undergraduate home in the Melton Hunt Cup.

The Cottenham race meeting remains the highlight of the Cambridge University sporting calendar. Undergraduates are specifically implicated in two races, the United Hunts Club Members Race and the United Hunts Club Past and Present. Recent honorary secretaries of the United Hunts Club, Major E.W.R. Bolden, and the brothers Anthony and Peter Pemberton (of Trumpington Hall) as well as James Midgeley, the present secretary, are notable for the efficiency with which meetings have been organised, and for the fact that over the last few years their efforts have resulted in record entries. But what brings the greatest satisfaction to the membership of the Trinity Foot Beagles is that the point-to-point continues to cement the bond of custom and friendship between the beagles and the town of Cottenham. As long as this bond survives the pack is guaranteed access to excellent hunting country within a few miles of Cambridge, as well as to a marvellous variety of pastime and good company.

CHAPTER FOUR

THE SPORTING CANTAB

At the beginning of almost every hunting year a new master of the TFB takes office. He is chosen by his predecessor; and the qualities necessary for the job are as much enthusiasm and sociability as experience of hunting hounds. The first two are essential if the master is to win undergraduate support, without which it is impossible to run the pack. Inexperience of hunting hounds has never proved insuperable: most masters come from a sporting or country background, which enables them to pick up the techniques of hare hunting fairly quickly. The all-pervasive atmosphere of Cambridge reduces the need further, for it is conducive to the life of the dilettante and the gifted amateur. The effect this has upon a master of hounds is that it adds a humourous detachment to his otherwise serious intentions. He determines to kill hares, but cares little for his tally; he breeds hounds to hunt, but not to show; he aims to show sport and by so doing give pleasure to himself, his followers and friends. Masters who do not fall under this spell and who seek to impose rigid professional standards on the TFB have often been disappointed. For it is not a smart school pack in a fashionable country; it has hardly any "county" support and even less financial security. For many years there have been only two regular followers from outside the university. They are Colonels Hugh and Neil Fraser. Their loyalty and enthusiasm has always been greatly appreciated. Therefore, the outlook and personality of the master and his whips is all important and explains why the TFB has survived for so long.

Since R.G. Hoare first hunted his pack in 1862 there have been over one hundred masters of beagles in Cambridge. At first sight it would seem impossible to trace any evidence of continuity running throughout such a mob, but R.G. Hoare provides the clue. For his family, along with two others, the Barclays and the Buxtons, produced innumerable masters and whips during the Victorian and Edwardian era of this history. All three families were Quaker by background, all three came from East Anglia, and – most important of all – all three were kin. The blood of other families, such as the Wiggins and the Holland-Hibberts, also courses through the strain of TFB masters; and each season with the advent of another generation, family connections are revived. During the author's mastership one of his most

48

assiduous whips was Robert Gladstone, whose grandfather, H.S. Gladstone, had been master in 1899. Robert hunted in the green velvet coat of his grandfather, which thereby had its first airing in the fens for seventy-four years. The TFB has become for many families a tradition, strengthened by the kinship and friendship between the masters and whips of each generation.

It is unrecorded what the Quaker patriach of the Hoare family thought of the activities of R.G. Hoare or those of his younger brother C.R.G. Hoare, who followed with W.E. Currey. But certainly C.R.G. Hoare can have had no grounds of complaint when his own son, David, became master in 1902. He came up from Harrow, where he must rank as the founder and possibly the only master of the Harrow beagles. For, whilst still at school, he kept four couple of hounds in a nearby farm, which hunted a drag and, when possible, hare.

In 1904 a representative from the senior branch of the Hoare family became master. This was C.G. Hoare, whose son, Bob Hoare, followed suit in 1930 and later became senior Trustee of the pack. When Bob Hoare was hunting the TFB in Northumberland in 1930 a journalist from one of the sporting papers was quick to note:

> That this Cambridge pack should spend the whole of September hunting in Northumberland is a very old tradition, and this year history is repeating itself more closely than usual for this season, master and huntsman Mr Bob Hoare, is son of Mr Christopher Hoare, the stockbroker, who hunted the pack in the same country some thirty years before.

Bob Hoare used his experience gained with the TFB well, and went on to become one of the most famous foxhunters of his generation. It is unfortunate that so far there has been no post-war representative of the Hoare family. Bob Hoare's sister married one of the most successful TFB masters of the 1920s, W.W. Hicks-Beach.

Interest in the TFB was first evinced by members of the Buxton family at the end of the 19th-century when two cousins, Gerald and Lewis (nicknamed "Mole") became whippers-in in 1882 and 1897. The first member of the family to rise to the heights of master was Anthony Buxton in 1903. Geoffrey Dent, a nephew of Anthony Buxton, although close in age, whipped in from 1912–13. He and his uncle, in the true Callaby tradition, shared a love of ratting. Anthony Buxton was so professional that on one occasion he was seen on Norwich station, after a visit to relatives, with a sackful of rats on his back: fresh stock to replenish that depleted by his terriers in Essex. A relative who whipped-in, in an unofficial capacity, to Anthony Buxton was Quentin, nicknamed Squinting, Gurney. He was so called because he once viewed the tired hare squatting at the end of a fenland drain.

Anthony Buxton started a pack of beagles in Switzerland whilst working with the League of Nations after the First World War. It would be hard to find a more unlikely beagling country, nor one which contrasted so strikingly with the fens. This period of his sporting career is described in his book *Sporting Interludes at Geneva*, published in 1932. Hares were extremely scarce in this part of Europe and Buxton unwittingly increased their rarity by hunting and killing the entire stock of fresh hares with which the Sociétè de Chasse were topping up the number which had survived the shooting season. This process was titled the "repeopling of the chase" by the Swiss.

To return to Edwardian Cambridge, another Buxton, Nigel, whipped-in during 1906; it is obvious from a drawing in the *Beagle Dinner Book* that he was as dedicated to foxhunting as he was to beagling, for it depicts him "undergoing an operation of trepanning as a result of an accident with the Fitzwilliam". His son, Mark, whipped-in in 1950. "Mole" Buxton's son became master in 1912 and Anthony's son, J.J. Buxton, in 1950, becoming the most recent member of the family to play a part in the running of the TFB. J.J. Buxton is related through his mother to the Stirlings, who produced W.J. Stirling as master in 1930 and to the Morlands, who produced C. Morland as master in 1959.

The Barclays of Brent Pelham have proved a continual source of encouragement to masters. They were also largely responsible for the preservation of the pack throughout both world wars. The first member to hunt with the pack was E.E. Barclay, who whipped in to Rowland Hunt. At the same time he also hunted his own harriers near Cromer in Norfolk and Higham in Suffolk. He was remembered by F.C. Kempson as:

> The best heavy-weight runner the writer ever saw – he stayed in the most wonderful manner, and one never seemed to be able to get on terms with him.

The same was also said about his nephew, H.G. Barclay (master 1902), whose brother J.F. Barclay whipped-in to him along with a distant relation, R.W. Barclay, (practically the whole hunt staff of 1902 were Barclays). In 1904, T.H. Barclay whipped-in; his first cousin A.L. Barclay was to become master in 1924. Maurice and Geoffrey, sons of E.E. Barclay, were both masters (1907–08 and 1912–13 respectively). Geoffrey was another famous Barclay heavy-weight runner who once, when hunting the Eton College Hunt in 1909, had to be pulled out of a ditch by George Champion, leaving his boots behind. Both brothers fought in the First World War, Maurice taking twenty two of the Puckeridge Hunt horses with him; and Geoffrey, who was killed in 1916, his hunting horn. Their sister married Captain Edward Charles Dimsdale, whose two sons, Tom and John, were also masters (1931–32 and 1933–34 respectively). The most recent member to hunt the TFB was Charlie Barclay, son of Maurice. He was master for a brief period in 1939 and returned after the war to whip-in to Alan Baxter. However, his allegiance was soon claimed by the Puckeridge Hunt and in 1947 he became joint-master with his father and grandfather: a triumvirate, which spanned sixty-nine years of the TFB history and fifty-one of Puckeridge history.

Against this pattern of kinship must be added that of friendship, which is founded upon the social activities of the Beagle Club. The club is the tangible bond, which lends permanency to the succession of masters. It enshrines the traditions of the TFB and secures continuity in the way the pack is run. The club was founded for two reasons: to preserve the TFB's independence from both college and university authorities, and to channel the beaglers social instincts into a formal dining club.

Followers of the beagles had met socially after hunting since the days of the Foot Drag, when they used to meet to "wine" in each others' rooms after Hall, just as senior members of a college still have their wine and dessert after dinner in the senior combination room. For a short period in the 1870s this habit was formalised into a beagling wine club called the "Inseperables". Members (no doubt for convenience sake, as few men went out of their college after Hall) were confined to Trinity and their uniform was a plum coloured velvet jacket, with silver braid, the arms of Trinity and two clasped hands with the words *Quis Separabit*.

Gradually the fashion of wining after Hall died out. When Rowland Hunt was master he started having supper with his beagling friends on Sunday night. One evening he was forced to be absent, and explained to F.G. Howard who was a guest:

> I have asked the usual crowd, and one or two quiet freshmen who come out with the beagles that I want to be civil to.

All went well until supper was over when a full scale fight developed with various fruits serving as ammunition. When these ran out the 2 lb end of a tongue was fought over and used as a projectile. It narrowly missed the landlord (who put his head round the door because of the noise) and promptly split the door in two. It was last seen flying out of the window and landing in the midst of a group of people returning from evensong in the Round Church. So much for the quiet freshmen.

This tradition of supper in an undergraduate's room continued and it was natural that when the Beagle Club was formed in 1892 the rules should stipulate that the master and his whips should dine once a week in a member's rooms. After each dinner, at which members wore green velvet smoking jackets as set down in the rules, the events of the evening were minuted in the *Beagle Dinner Book*.

The first beagle dinner was held in Mr. Bowring's rooms and it is recorded that "there was some music and a small game of roulette." Up until the First World War the habit of meeting in a member's rooms or lodgings was continued. During Ralph Clark's mastership (1913–14) they met approximately once a fortnight. The dinner is always mentioned in his diary. For example:

> Nov. 8. Soham Mere. Fast pack. Third Beagle Dinner. Ralph Vane and Richardson hosts.

Unfortunately he does not elaborate on the proceedings of these dinners which on one occasion, when Geoffrey Dent was host in his lodgings at 12 Park Parade, included the concealment by Dent (for it will be remembered he was a great ratter) of some rats under a silver dish cover.

The tradition of dining in an undergraduate's rooms was common with many Cambridge University clubs in late-Victorian and Edwardian times. Even the committee of the Pitt Club (founded in 1835) dined in one another's rooms, for it was not until the creation of the Hoop Room in the Pitt Club in 1907 that private dinners could be held there at all.

After the First World War it was customary for the Beagle Club to hold their dinners in the Hoop Room; the sporting writer H.A. Bryden describes a typical dinner of the period:

> After an afternoon meet of the Trinity beagles on the last day of January 1923, which yielded one good hunt of an hour and ten minutes I dined by the invitation of W.H. Whitbread, still master of these hounds, with ten others of the hunt, at the Pitt Club one of the institutions of Cambridge. These hunt dinners take place some half a dozen times during the term and are rather special occasions. The members of the hunt wear green dinner jackets with silk facings. A Mr Pease, an undergraduate, was the only other guest. We had an elaborate and very good dinner, beginning with oysters and port wine, sherry, hock, burgundy, and some excellent port. Then came a few toasts and some hunting songs, among them John Peel and Drink Puppy Drink, with many a wild view halloa to follow. We adjourned at ten o'clock to the rooms of one of the members, where we played a

game of chance, for quite mild stakes, and were regaled with hot milk punch. At eleven came oysters and stout followed by whisky and soda for such as wanted it, and at twelve we broke up, and went our ways with more piercing view halloas which must have disturbed the dreams of many an adjacent sleeper. This was a most cheery function which I most enjoyed ... these young harehunters were as nice and cheery as you please; but there was none of that silly overdoing of hospitality which used to prevail in what are known as the Good Old Days.

Billy Whitbread can remember returning from one of these "cheery functions" with Dick Scrope. Scrope kept on halloaing and making a row, until one of the "adjacent sleepers" threw open his window in a rage, at which Dick Scrope cried excitedly: "Have you seen our fox?"

The Hoop Room has remained the most popular venue since those days and the number of toasts and ensuing escapades remain unabated. In the late 1920s and 1930s, after the blancmange in shape of a hare had been consumed, Bill Beattie, "the demon barber" from Jesus Lane, used to stand on the table and play popular tunes on his fiddle and later on members would hire a cab and, to the accompaniment of coach and hunting horns, drive up to the kennels to consume more port with Bob Floate.

The Hoop Room has witnessed many similar dinners since the last war, in which parlour games, singing and horn blowing competitions play a major part. Throughout, these have been characterised by as much good humour as high spirits, although this sense of bonhomie has often evaporated by the next morning, when many members have faced the flesh at the kennels with nausea, as they walked out hounds at dawn. Although the bill of fare naturally changes, jugged hare has long been a popular dish at such dinners. There is only one recorded incident of a member of the hunt actually eating raw hare. He was Willie Pryor, a whip to Michael Sclater in 1965. After a kill on Smithey Fen he got down amongst the hounds to sample a morsel of hare: he emerged triumphant and satiated with the words: "It had a hot, purplish taste."

The grandest and most sedate of all dinners took place at the Hyde Park Hotel in 1962, when a large number of past masters, followers and a few well chosen guests joined the hunt staff to celebrate the centenary of the pack. After the toast to the Queen the health of the TFB was proposed by Major M.E. Barclay (master 1906–8), with the reply being made by the then master, John Sclater. Hunting and the Guests were proposed by Viscount Knutsford (master 1940) which were replied to by the Duke of Beaufort MFH for Hunting and Captain Ronnie Wallace MFH for the Guests.

On occasions it has been known for these dinners to get out of hand, threatening danger to the very fabric of the Pitt Club and nearby colleges. Attempts at destruction are usually brought to a sudden halt with the viewing of porters and proctors who unite in their attempts to overtake and apprehend the all too swift greenbacks. Proctors interrupted such escapades most frequently during the 1920s and 1930s when there were more rules to break than there are now. One such rule demanded that all undergraduates should be in their rooms after midnight. Baron Dimsdale describes what happened to W.J. Stirling when he once tried to evade this law:

> Towards the end of the Lent term it seemed a good plan to Bill to enter Trinity by the Great Gate then climb out and go in at the gate again so that the Porter's book read 10.10 Mr. Stirling, 10.20 Mr. Stirling etc. He probably refreshed himself in his room during each circuit till he eventually hooked himself up by the heel on some spikes from which the proctor had to unhook him. For this he was gated and threw such a party in his room that he fell against the wall and concussed himself. For a time he carried on hunting with a poisoned heel and concussion, but then even he had to give in and I took over for a time.
>
> W.J. Stirling went on to found the S.A.S. during the Second World War.

On another occasion Michael Dill was caught coming back from a dinner after midnight: "I was progged in All Saints Passage, infuriating." The sequel to the event is described a few pages later in his diary:

> I went to see Mr. ****, one of the proctors, I found him in a very nice panelled room in Nevile's Court with a delightful moulded ceiling. I was struck and felt that here must live a representative of the old port drinking type of culture and learning. A second look at the furniture gave me doubts however and Mr. **** shattered my hopes. He was a little man with large ARP badge glasses, black hair and a rather garbled form of the King's English. As soon as I began to speak to him he showed that he had a mean outlook so characteristic of the new learning. I gave up my 6/8 with all grace, and we parted cordially ...

Most members of the Beagle Club are automatically members of the Cambridge University United Hunts Club. Apart from running the point-to-point, the club also stages the Hunt Ball every year.

Before the First World War this was held at the Guildhall and Ralph Clarke, who organised it in 1913, recorded in his diary: "The beagle ball went off quite well and made £23 on 117 tickets."

Between the wars the Hunt Ball was held in the University Arms Hotel. In 1952 John Stourton broke with tradition by holding the ball in November and in the Pitt Club. He made £220 profit from the dance with tickets at 30s., and champagne at 27s. 6d., a bottle. The timing and venue of the ball has remained the same ever since.

In 1969 and 1970 there was a new departure, never since repeated, in the type of entertainment offered at the ball, by the arrival of a "strip tease artiste", who came on stage dressed as a traffic warden. She enjoyed it so much that she came back the following year – free. Freddie Markham, who dealt with her at the time, describes her stationery as having all her prizes and achievements, such as, "Crowned Miss Cinema of the East Midlands 1953", printed round the edge.

The Ball gives members the opportunity to don their distinguished evening dress which consists of a green tail coat with dark blue velvet collar, white silk facings and a buff waistcoat. A social diarist remarked on the coat at the Devon and Somerset Hunt Ball in 1930:

> A gold braided pink coat from France-stood out amongst its English relations, and Mr. Hoare's green one could not be missed either. He is the master of the Trinity Foot Beagles and has lately had them at his home at Exford, the Quarme Harriers having permitted them to hunt their country for four days a week.

Until the Second World War and the contraction of social life in Cambridge, the university consisted of a number of totally different worlds, reflected in the large number of university clubs in existence. Most members of the Beagle Club have been members of the Pitt Club. [It has to be recorded that one President of the Beagle Club has actually been expelled from the Pitt – for blowing up the band at the Pitt Club Ball by throwing a thunderflash down the tuba.] In the 19th-century a few were also members of the Hawks Club and over the years a few have been members of the Athanaeum. This club had originally started as a debating society with membership restricted to those from the higher strata of society. Originally they used to meet for teas, but later, in their club rooms which looked onto Trinity Great Gate, they met neither to debate nor to drink tea, as an incident that occurred during the 1920s shows. In the middle of an afternoon the windows of the club were suddenly thrown open by an exuberant member, who proceeded to pour champagne onto the heads below shouting "Bolly for the plebs".

Few beaglers have been members of this club. The strongest links between the Beagle and Athanaeum clubs were formed in 1920 when Gilbert Dunning and Billy Whitbread (masters 1914–21 and 1921–23 respectively) were members. They elected a number of beaglers to the Athanaeum and an album, entitled the Beagle and Athanaeum Club exists of groups photographed during this period. It was during the 1920s that the TFB went up in the world: Prince George (later King George VI) and Prince Henry (later Duke of Gloucester) occasionally came out.

Members of the TFB have also found time to beagle with other packs. Twice they have made visits to the Christ Church. The first time, in 1936, J.J. Mann organised a party. The event is recorded in his diary:

> Charlton-on-Otmoor Dec 21st Christ Church Beagles 2 p.m. Invading party that went in my car were Rodney (Howe), Bryce (Knox), Denis (Freeman) and myself. We started as usual in a great hurry and late so we had to thrash along a bit, but we got there in very nice time so we were able to inspect the standard of the Oxford beagles. Drew onto Otmoor, which when not used for beagling is a bomber ground, these seemed its only two possibilities of usefulness it was a wet waste of long lank grass growing on ridge and furrow.
>
> It was some time before a hare got up. But when it did hounds hunted really toppingly and really worked like blazes as scent was not very good. They killed after 1 hour and 25 minutes square in the open. She was properly beat up. We each got a trophy, I the mask. It was a small hare but a tough one.

On the second occasion, the TFB went to the Christ Church, they took their hounds with them. J.R. Sclater, master from 1960–61, was hunting and it was the last day of his mastership. Unfortunately the day ended with hounds running into a wood. Only on one occasion has the visit been returned when J. Walters who was master of the Christ Church in 1966, came out and was given the horn as they moved off.

Another pack that has been connected with the Trinity Foot is the Bolebrooke. This link was also established by J.J. Mann whose father, Percy Mann, founded them. It was only natural that Jock should have been given the chance of hunting them and he did so during one vacation in 1936 when he hunted a triplicate pack consisting of five couple from each of the following packs: the TFB, the Bolebroke and the Brissenden. The experiment was only partially successful owing to the noise of the field and hounds not knowing one another.

The connection between the two packs was revived by J.R. Sclater, who hunted the Bolebroke for a week in Northumberland in 1964.

During the Christmas vacations, masters usually take some hounds home with them to hunt. This tradition was begun in 1902 by Anthony Buxton. Since then the TFB have made expeditions throughout Britain including: Taunton in 1930, where, according to one witness, the locals thought beagles hunted beavers in water; Worcestershire, during Brandon Cadbury's mastership; Romney Marsh in Jock Mann's mastership; to Exmoor again during Rex Hancock's and John Kirkpatrick's mastership; to Horsey in Norfolk during John Buxton's mastership; to Northamptonshire during Michael Parry's mastership; to Surrey during Stephen Lambert's mastership and to the North Riding of Yorkshire during Tom Ramsden's mastership.

These expeditions were exhausting sporting tours. In Geoffrey Dent's day they hunted every day except Christmas when, predictably, he went ratting; and at Horsey, home of Anthony Buxton (the coldest house in Europe where the inhabitants are reputed to have protective plumage like seafowl), they rose at four to flight duck, beagled all day and flighted again at dusk. In the vacations beaglers also organised foxhunting expeditions to Ireland, the Shires and occasionally Scotland. Jock Mann did the latter in 1937 when he had a day with the Dumfriesshire. He wrote after a hunt from Hoddam: "Sir Jock Buchanan-Jardine had an opportunity to use his iron crop and smashed two railway gates with it."

Members of the TFB have always worked as little or as hard as they want to, and nearly all leave Cambridge with degrees. Indeed a number have gained First Class Honours. The gilded youth before the First World War produced three from their midst: Ralph Clarke, Geoffrey Dent and William de Geijar. Perhaps the most distinguished first of recent years was that of John Sclater who also killed the record number of hares (43$\frac{1}{2}$ brace), as well as provided historic sport in both Cambridge and Northumberland.

For those beaglers who have not taken their work so seriously the Easter Term has been one devoted to otter hunting and occasionally rowing. R.H. Studholme (master in 1923) records in 1922:

> Became secretary of TFB thus holding the unique position of being secretary of third Trinity and Trinity Foot Beagles ...

... and in the 1930s there was a beagle eight which took part in the Bumps. During the 1930s a trencher fed bobbery pack was also formed, it consisted of one greyhound, one dachshund, one border terrier, one spaniel and two smooth fox terriers. Their bag consisted of rabbits, field mice and grass snakes. The meets took place in the fens, and were sometimes preceded by a cockfight.

The unacademic activities of one master, Michael Sclater, gained prominence in 1965, when a team of reporters from *The Sunday Times* descended upon Cambridge to find out how members of the university spent their day. Michael Sclater was not in when the reporter called and his empty rooms were described as follows:

> Outside the room of the master of the Trinity Foot Beagles were two drakes spread out on the coat pegs and hanging below them, two ducks. Their blood had dripped and dried dark green on the new bathtub beneath. Under the bath were a pair of muddy beagling shoes. Both doors to his room were open, gas fire blazing, a pair of white trousers drying in front of it over a chair. On the mantelpiece were two empty and one full bottle of the college's own superior dry sherry, with the college crest on the label. A dull copper horn stood upright, by the door, and in the middle of the table another in silver, shinier, but a bit dented.

A few days later the reporter received a letter from the master's personal secretary giving details of his day. It read as follows:

> Dear Sir,
> Michael Sclater has asked me to write in reply to your letter of October 17, 1966 to say that if your cross section was to be of working members of the university you may well have written to the wrong person. The outline of his day was as follows: 10–12 noon dealt with correspondence; 12–1.30 lunch in the Pitt Club; 1.30 exercised the hounds and organised at the Kennels; 3–6 slept; dinner in the Pitt Club and an early night. We hope this may be of some help to you.
> Yours faithfully,
> Ann Davidson. (Secretary).

At the same time the Secretary of the Anti-Field Sports League was also visited and the following interview took place:

> The Secretary of the Cambridge anti-hunt society is a student of the tribes of Madagascar. He has been there himself, and if he gets his Ph.D., would like to be employed by some African Government in a research and advisory capacity (for example a long-term investigation of the social problems involved in setting up a factory or township in a primitive area).

All afternoon the Secretary was researching in his college library for an essay on "Social Control among the Arushi Tribes in Tanzania". Obviously the tribes of Africa took up much of his time for the TFB received little harassment from this group.

A few senior members of the University have consistently supported the TFB, most notably Professor Clark-Kennedy, Senior Fellow of Corpus Christi, who, although advanced in years and short of sight continues to hunt with the pack. Apart from beagling he has pursued a varied sporting career from skating on the Zuider Zee to stalking puffins on Ailsa Craig. In the 1950s another keen supporter was Professor Vincent, Professor of Italian and also a Fellow of Corpus Christi.

Involvement with the Trinity Foot Beagles has never been known to hinder a man's career: the number of ex-masters, whips and followers in positions of responsibility is evidence of this; and certainly in the field of foxhunting it has proved the key to success. One reason for this is that most TFB masters came from foxhunting backgrounds so that even when hunting with beagles, their technique is based more upon the principles of fox as opposed to hare hunting. Almost certainly they have been brought up (along with so many other English children) on the three classic books on foxhunting: *Thoughts on Hunting* by Peter Beckford (1781); *Diary of a Huntsman* by Tom Smith (1838); and *Hunting the Fox* by Lord Willoughby de Broke (1920). They are conversant with these long before they set eyes on those great books on beagling by Otho Paget, and certainly long before they read other textbooks of a more academic nature.

But apart from gaining the invaluable experience of running and hunting a pack of hounds, the one overriding experience of all ex-masters and followers is what supreme fun the TFB was. The most important reason for this must lie in the type of person it attracts. Alfred Gilbey, who, as Chaplain to the Catholic undergraduates, was resident in Cambridge for exactly 100 terms, and a devoted beagler throughout that period, supplies the best definition of the Cambridge beagler:

> The TFB discovers the people with naturally country backgrounds and in the days when there were those with a lot of money, it attracted those without too much. People have been known to hunt and play polo for secondary reasons, but never has anyone been known to beagle for any other reason than that they like beagling. I always cherish the illusion that all beaglers are the sons of country parsons, in fact I cannot think of a single one that was.

CHAPTER FIVE

THE NATION AT WAR

In spite of John Jorrocks describing hunting as "the image of War without its guilt, and only five and twenty per cent of its danger!" the two world wars covered by this short history presented hunting with almost insuperable problems. During the First and Second World Wars, foxhunting was recognised by the Ministry of Agriculture as being the most efficient method of controlling the fox population, and there were sufficient middle aged hunt servants and foxhunters, too old for active service, who were available to maintain small establishments in most countries with the modest aim of fox destruction. During the Second World War a small allocation of petrol was available to most hunts for the purpose of pest control.

Hare hunting was much more difficult to justify and packs of beagles survived only by the dedication of a few elderly supporters, whose main justification was to provide sport for the hard worked countrymen and farmers, and exercise for those serving with the armed forces. The school packs were maintained on a much reduced scale, and could provide sufficient staff, but the university packs were to fare badly with the increasing call to the colours of this age group, and an ever decreasing number of undergraduates capable or willing to devote time to beagling.

With a dwindling subscription list and a shortage of flesh the future of the Trinity Foot Beagles looked bleak.

It is to the few who made it their business to work for the survival of the TFB in both wars that this chapter is dedicated. It is to them that we raise our cap.

On May 1st, 1914, G.K. Dunning took over the mastership from R.S. Clarke, and officially he remained master for six seasons – the longest single mastership in the history of the hunt. In fact he immediately joined the army on the outbreak of war in August, 1914, and Mr. E.H. Parker, a trustee, took charge of the hounds. He was joined by Mr. E.E. Barclay – both of whom ensured the survival of the pack for the next four years. In 1914 the hounds left their kennels in Cambridge, to be hunted by a group of sporting officers in the Welsh Division, and in 1915 they were moved to Seaford, to provide sport for a battalion of the Kings Royal Rifles. The TFB returned to Cambridge in 1916.

without master, staff or funds. A debt to the tune of £200 increased the difficulties, but an appeal – launched by Mr. E.H. Parker and Mr. N.O. Walker – resulted in the handsome sum of £760. Many ex-masters and supporters contributed to the appeal – including seven Barclays, five Buxtons, three Holland-Hibberts, two Hoares and two Wiggins.

By now many ex-TFB men were on active service, including those who had already served in the Boer War. The two most famous casualties of this generation were Clement Mitford (master 1897), heir to the first Lord Redesdale; and G.A. Boyd-Rochfort (whip 1899) who won a posthumous Victoria Cross in France in 1915. The immediate pre-war undergraduates who beagled during Ralph Clarke's mastership enlisted immediately and by 1916 the majority were listed as casualties. These included Geoffrey Bolitho, Dick Davies, Roy Mackenzie and Sidney Barthrop.

While E.E. Barclay was doing so much to preserve the TFB, his son G.W. Barclay, who carried the horn during the 1912 season, was killed in action, displaying at all times the courage and initiative expected from a Trinity Foot master. The last letter which he wrote to his mother expressed the feelings of so many of his generation:

> Dearest Mother
> There is a big push on now and I am going up to the front line, having been with the reinforcements. If I don't get through I am telling Baker to send you this hurried scrawl. I am very well and happy and I know that I could not end my life a better way.

He was killed by a sniper while visiting his soldiers in the trenches.

In 1919 the fortunes of the TFB began to look up. G.K. Dunning survived the war and returned to Cambridge to renew his mastership, "as a man", in H.A. Bryden's words, "of ripe experience and great judgement". He was from all accounts a formidable figure and it is largely thanks to his personality and experience that the pack recovered so quickly.

Whilst at Eton he had been master of the Eton College Hunt, where he broke what was then the record for the number of hares killed. He accounted for 33 hares and one fox in 45 hunting days. He was also keeper of the Field and the Wall, No. 6 batsman in the First Eleven and winner of the school steeplechase.

He hunted the TFB for two consecutive seasons, which was undoubtedly a great advantage both to himself and the pack. He had two whippers-in, J.D. Harrison and W.H. Whitbread, and a deputy master V.J.B. Seely.

The appointment of a deputy master was, and still is, unique with the TFB but was necessary as a result of an illness contracted by G.K. Dunning in

Mesopotamia, which prevented him from swimming. When levels or drains had to be crossed the horn was passed to Victor Seely, who was forced to swim while the master (true to the words of H.A. Bryden) sought the nearest bridge.

As secretary of the Pitt Club Dunning was largely responsible for the revival of this establishment after the war. His obituary included mention of his Cambridge days:

> It was extraordinary how his strength of character and integrity influenced his circle of sporting friends at the University and I suppose it was complete straightness and his sense of humour that made up such a lovable personality.

Between the wars once the hurdle of little-go had been surmounted it was possible with a modest allowance to keep a hunter at livery and to hunt two or more days a week, as well as to beagle. There was any amount of sport to choose from. The Cambridgeshire Harriers under Richard Barlow attracted large fields. The pack was owned by John Towler, a farmer, who had been master from 1914–22 and from 1931–32. Since then he had acted as honorary secretary and kennelled the hounds at his home, Tunbridge Hall near Bottisham. Richard Barlow hunted them whilst still an undergraduate and then immediately after he came down from 1934–36. The Cambridgeshire Harriers had always had close ties with the university, as early as 1828 an undergraduate of Emmanuel, Charles Bennett, was hunting a pack in this country and, since 1891 when W.B. Austin was master, there had been a series of undergraduate masters. He was a great friend of all the beaglers of that generation and on one occasion he even acquired the assistance of the then master J.J. Mann, to hunt roe deer with his Harriers in one of the Cambridgeshire coverts. Michael Dill (master in 1940) enjoyed a more conventional day's sport with them, which took place after a hunt ball and exhibits his enthusiasm for sport:

> Up at 7.45 only getting $4^1/_2$ hours sleep ... went and told Grierson [his tutor] I could only see him on some other day. ... (I had had a bath and changed into my breeches and boots with grey flannels over) ... picked up my bowler, spurs etc., which I had left at Sidney Smith's [tailors] went off to Cap Harris's yard. He was just leaving. I got on Tipsy Toaster and trotted off to catch him up. The Harriers met at Fen Ditton and we hunted all round Quy Station ... I was back in my digs before 3.30 so I decided to bike out to Waterman and see how the TFB were doing. I got there in good time to find John Stubber hunting

hounds ... had two good hunts and lost two tired hares ... that night hunt dinner.

Michael Dill's brother, Richard was up at Cambridge for a period during the war, when he hunted the Harriers.

The Cambridgeshire and the Fitzwilliam were the nearest foxhound packs, and for £5 subscription per term the undergraduate could hunt with either as often as he liked. The Fitzwilliam was the more fashionable of the two packs, where the huntsman, Tom Agutter was at his peak, and the country was strongly fenced and free of plough and wire. Undergraduates and their hirelings used to travel to the meets by train. One TFB master who hunted regularly with the Fitzwilliam was J.J. Mann. He would leap the fen ditches on foot one day and face up to the bullfinches of the Fitzwilliam, on the next.

Inspired no doubt by days such as these the beagler occasionally tried his hand at mounted beagling. The last occasion when all the field was mounted was in 1939 when they caused chaos by hunting wildly through a prize stud at Newmarket. In 1930 they received an even greater fright when Bob Hoare was caught drawing one of the Cambridgeshire coverts at Swavesey. Luckily it was only by the second horseman coming home and not by the master, Douglas Crossman, who could be terrifying when roused.

In May 1939 John Milburn, who also had his own private pack, the Guyzance, became master. That September he took them to his home county of Northumberland, where as usual both sportsmen and hounds enjoyed the hospitality of Nicholas Beveridge at the Bridge of Aln Hotel. On September 1st, hounds met at Hartside, in a fog and had a disappointing morning. Charlie Barclay who was whipping-in described the events that followed in his hunting diary:

> When we got back to the Bridge of Aln after beagling this morning we learnt that Germany had invaded Poland, which means that England is bound to be at war in a few days time. This being the case we decided to have a last go and we took out both the TFB pack and the Guyzance pack $(45^1/_2)$ couple in all [in fact it was 52 couple]. Found several hares in a large patch of roots beside the River Coquet below the gardens of the Hall, but we failed to get away so we did no good ... finally worked up to a beaten hare at back of Guyzance kennels and hounds ran slap along hedge of the gardens up to the steep bank of the river. Got up to our hare here and ran over the bend of the river our hare went down the bank to the wooded path she turned left handed for a bit, and hounds ran with a really wonderful cry which echoed

and echoed and ran slap into her on the path. A magnificent finish to a historic evening's sport. A fine tonic hunting is!

On September 2nd, John Milburn, already a Territorial Army officer left to join the Northumberland Hussars, affectionately known as "The Noodles".

In Cottenham it was a different story. As hounds were pursuing Northumberland hares through the woods of Guyzance – the local policeman, P.C. Haines, proceeded down the Cottenham High Street blowing his whistle – to announce the outbreak of war. Ralph Norman's old uncle employed an even older housekeeper, who was taken by surprise by such unprecedented behaviour in the High Street, and at the call of the whistle rushed out of the house attired only in her nightdress. P.C. Haines delivered a suitable reprimand, after which, still in her nightdress, she reappeared wearing a gas mask.

The undergraduates were not totally unprepared for war and many had enlisted in the Cambridge University O.T.C. Cavalry Squadron. Parades took place on the rifle range – within sight of the TFB kennels – at 7 a.m. in the morning. At this early hour some members of the squadron were not fully awake, and on one occasion John Milburn was challenged to lark over a stiff obstacle. Thinking that he was mounted on his usual patent safety he set sail and suffered a crashing fall. His horse in fact was a newcomer to the squadron, young, unschooled and very green. The price paid was 6 stitches and 14 days in the Evelyn Nursing Home.

Charlie Barclay took over from John Milburn who had enjoyed only one week as huntsman. His secretary was Michael Dill and his first whip Julian Holland-Hibbert. His term as master was extremely short, and his last day was at Rampton on December 7th.

> Only Hereward the Wake, John Hamilton-Stubber and another out. We drew miles of country without really getting onto a hare though hounds spoke to line occasionally ... My last days hunting with the TFB as I go to the 3rd Cavalry Training Regiment at Weedon tomorrow. We have had a fairly successful terms beagling though our bag is somewhat meagre.

His departure was greeted with consternation by his staff. The situation was complicated by the fact that Michael Dill, his most likely successor, was already committed to the running of the Pitt Club and the Whip club. He felt inexperienced in the post of master, but there seemed no one else available to take on the hounds. In the end both he and Julian Holland-Hibbert agreed to become masters.

Wartime beagling in Cambridge in September 1940. (*From left to right*) Bob Floate, junior, Michael Hewitt, Captain Monckton (now Major-General the Viscount Monckton), John Milburn (now Sir John Milburn, Bt., MFH), Miss Butcher (now Lady Milburn), Father A.N. Gilbey (now Monsignor A.N. Gilbey), Baron W. Gelsey Gutmann, unidentified.

The first three months of 1940 proved to be very difficult for the hunt – quite apart from the military setbacks of the war. Frost and snow in January and February confined hounds to kennels, and skating on Newnham Meadows provided beaglers with the only form of exercise. Then in February a fire destroyed half the buildings at the kennels. Michael Dill wrote in his diary: "Lunched at the Pitt Club and then went off to inspect the kennels. The fire has gutted about half the buildings. I hope to goodness the insurance company will agree to pay up or else God knows!" Later that month they held their first meet of the term in terrible conditions. Large snow drifts remained and the country was waterlogged with slush. To add to the hazards, an outbreak of foot and mouth disease confined hunting to the environs of Cambridge. The joint masters held their last meet of the season at the Jolly Waterman. It was a great day and hounds screamed to the outskirts of Milton Michael Dill wrote:

> So ended our last day as joint masters of the TFB. It was with deep regret that I doffed my green cap for the last time. One can only hope for a good season next year in spite of the war.

Arrangements for season 1940–41 were completed when John Hamilton-Stubber was appointed Master. On Hitler's birthday, 20th April, he, Michael Dill, Ian Macrill, Patrick Dickson and Hereward the Wake inspected the young entry at the kennels. The German invasion of Holland and Belgium cast a further shadow over the future of the TFB and, in July 1940, the master was called up, leaving the establishment in the ever-willing hands of M.E Barclay. Like his father in the First World War, he was to be the saviour of the hunt during the Second.

However, the TFB were destined to hunt for another season from their kennels. By a curious quirk of fortune, John Milburn with the Northumberland Hussars, found himself stationed at Fowlmere. This provided him with an admirable opportunity to hunt hounds, which had previously been snatched from him by the little corporal. He provided sport and exercise for large numbers of Yeomen, many of whom preferred beagling to organised games.

Gilbert Monckton, a survivor of Dunkirk, was stationed at Cambridge. He also became a staunch supporter as in pre-war days. The most notable hunt took place from Comberton. They put up an old dog fox and ran him straight into the village and up into the rafters of a house, next door to a house where a man was supposedly dying. In good fashion they had their fox (the Cambridgeshire were quite happy about it) and the man survived. It was only later that John Milburn discovered that the Brigadier and staff were all out including the ex-TFB deputy master, Victor Seely. That night the messing officer, Billy Williamson, by the light of oil lamps concocted the following verse:

> *In matters of hunting the charm of the Noodles*
> *Is slaying old Charlie with Trinity Poodles*
> *We're sorry you wer'nt there to see the good sport,*
> *And drown our ennui in bloody bad port.*

With the outbreak of war the sporting and social life of Cambridge had naturally contracted, and there were two clubs which became intimately connected with the TFB: the Whip Club and the Interim Club.

The Whip Club had been founded by Gilbert Monckton in 1938. Twenty two rules of the club were drawn up, the most important being:

> That the object of the Club be to encourage the sport and art of driving, and to further the more general use of the horse.

It was founded at a time when horses were readily available, nearly every tradesman had a horse and there were a number of thriving livery stables, such as Tom Elwood's or Calham's stables opposite the Fitzwilliam Museum. Calham claimed to have once been the coachman of a minor German princeling, a status only matched by the barrowman by the Round Church who claimed to be the illegitimate son of Edward VII.

The outbreak of war brought with it severe petrol rationing, which provided impetus and a new lease of life to the Whip Club. In November *Horse and Hound* reported:

> It was feared that when war broke out the Club would have to be closed down for the duration and when the new term began at Cambridge the Club was, in fact, reduced to one driving member and four other undergraduate members. However owing to the support which we have received, the Club is now almost up to pre-war establishment. Owing to the restriction on petrol the Club has been of considerable practical use to the members who own turn outs. One of the Club governor's carts often takes the hounds of the Trinity Foot Beagles on their furthest meets.

Throughout the winter of 1939 both the beagles and the Whip Club were sustained by the enthusiasm of Michael Dill. He drove everywhere. He arranged meets with the help of Taylor's dog cart:

I had lunch in hall and then bicycled down to the White's stables, where Charlie (Barclay) and I were taken in Taylor's dog cart to Girton ...

He drove to meets:

I took John (Cole). Our pony extremely slow and soon we were overhauled by Charlie (Barclay) with lots of hounds in the tub and then by Tibby (Taylor) with the rest. There was a good field considering the cold and the distance of 20 Pence Bridge!

He also took puppies to the train by gig, on one occasion with disastrous results:

I went up to the kennels and exercised hounds with Charlie (Barclay) and Tibby (Taylor) and Hereward (the Wake) and then we put my puppies in a tea chest ... it was dark by the time I started out and on the way up to the station we had two narrow shaves. I got hold of a boy to hold the horse and took in the box to the parcels office. Of course it took ages, but eventually I got it all settled. When I got outside the trap had disappeared. I got hold of the police and they eventually told me it had been apprehended at the War Memorial crossing undriven in the traffic. They let me off but I fear evil consequences.

The Interim Club was established with the idea of expanding the Whip Club, to allow it to take over the role of the Pitt, which had closed at the outbreak of war and was shortly to become a British Restaurant. In addition, the Interim took over the Athanaeum Rooms looking onto Trinity Street, where tea, reminiscent of the early years of the Athanaeum, was served every afternoon. All the Whip Club relics and records were housed in the Interim and prominent members of the Whip Club such as Q (Sir Arthur Quiller Couch) and Alfred Gilbey were regular attenders. Michael Dill partook of the first Interim Tea:

Went off to the Interim Club for Tea. David Cambell, David Mallick, John Bolton Carter, Jarnius Woodsend, John Stubber, Tibby Taylor, were those present for the first Interim tea and a good meal it was too ...

The military and naval disasters during 1940 probably encouraged undergraduates to make the most of their lives while at Cambridge. Michael

Michael Dill, joint master during the extremely difficult season of 1939–40. He was also secretary of the Whip Club and founder member of the Interim Club.

Dill's splendid diary reports fully on hunting, shooting, skating, dancing, dining and theatricals – paying scant attention to serious work. No doubt the thoughts of future campaigning against the Germans made light hearted pleasures more readily grasped. Michael Dill was killed in Italy while serving with his regiment the 16th/5th Lancers – which formed part of the famous 6 Armoured Division, the divisional sign of which was the mailed fist. In every Cambridge college the rolls of honour are studded with the names of beaglers, which include Michael Bell, Ian Blacker, Piers Edgcumbe and Ian Anderson, to mention only a few. In Michael Dill's kit bag the following poem was found, which refers to his short but lively fortunes at Cambridge:

> *I will call it the age of the Gilbertines**
> *As in truth he was leader of all*
> *As he rode at the head of the cavalry*
> *Or answered the roads subtle call*
>
> *As we drove to the Two Thousand Guineas,*
> *As we hatched some new plot in the Bath,†*
> *Then Gilbert was ever the leader,*
> *The stalwart who showed us the path.*
>
> *Yet he was but one of so many*
> *Of the best of good friends in the world*
> *Though they might have been guilty of any*
> *Of the storm of abuse that was hurled*
>
> *Their weakness was perfectly human*
> *Their foibles were clear to the eye,*
> *But their qualities stirling outbalanced*
> *Any wrongs their opponents might cry.*
>
> *When we finished a day with the beagles*
> *Neath the shadow of Cottenham Tower,*
> *As we listened to Walter and Horace*
> *Or toasted the countryman's power.*
>
> *As the roar of the cannon grows louder*
> *And there's more of us plunged in the fray*
> *And our allies are crumbling to powder*
> *I fear for the price we shall pay.*

* Named after Gilbert Monckton. † The Bath Hotel

In 1941 no undergraduate was available to accept the mastership or to maintain the hounds and Major Barclay on behalf of the trustees lent the hounds to a territorial battalion of the Hampshire Regiment. Mr. Frank Mitchell an officer in the battalion hunted the pack until 1944.

During this time Major Barclay lost trace of the hounds but, by an advertisement in *Horse and Hound* (which maintained publication throughout the war) they were discovered in Kent. A further advertisement for a huntsman was answered by John Parry serving with the 62nd Reconnaissance Training Regiment in Catterick. In a remarkable way his commanding officer happened to be the famous W.H. Whitbread (master 1921–22) who, when approached, expressed surprise and delivered a raspberry at John Parry's request to take on the hounds – but only for a moment. Permission was, of course, willingly granted.

John Parry collected the hounds from a gunner regiment in Sheerness which involved getting them across London in a taxi and buying sixteen "Dog" tickets from St. Pancras to Yorkshire.

For two seasons, 1944–45 and 1945–46, the merry voice of the TFB rang out in some of the finest hunting country in the North Riding. Mid-week, the meets were in the Zetland country and on Saturdays they hunted in Swaledale or Wensleydale. The first whipper-in was P.F. Marriner (later to become huntsman of the Claro beagles) and other members of his staff included the distinguished artist Michael Lyne and Luke Seymour. Drafts of four couple from the United Cotswold beagles (Michael Lyne's old pack) and $1^1/_2$ couple from the Tees Valley enlarged the pack. Experience of Northumberland hunting being obscured by the lapse of time, the TFB hounds had difficulty in surmounting the stone walls, but they soon acquired the taste for these obstacles and in a splendid scenting country they provided wonderful sport.

In 1945 large numbers of servicemen who had been prisoners of the Japanese arrived in Catterick. For them following the beagles proved to be "the greatest tonic" as suggested in the diary of Charlie Barclay. Today in the bar of the Punch Bowl in Reith, near Richmond, there hangs a photograph as a reminder of this period in the history of the TFB. It was in the Punch Bowl that the staff of the TFB (Yorkshire) met the local farmers in true Cambridge tradition. Michael Lyne produced a picture of hounds on Reithlow Moor and a sketch of the kennels.

Before the Second World War, John Parry had been whipper-in to the Dudley-Smith beagles which hunted in Dumfriesshire. War-time in Yorkshire forced him to forget this training and adopt an unorthodox style of kennel management. The kennels were nissen huts and, as with most packs kept by the army, hounds were fed on swill from the cookhouse. The hound van was a home-made trailer towed by a 15 cwt. truck.

When the beagles left their Cambridge kennels in 1941, Bob Floate, their kennel huntsman, was sent to Doncaster to train bloodhounds, where he rose to the rank of aircraftman.

In Cottenham the locals joined the Home Guard, and would have presented a fearsome body of men had the Germans been foolish enough to cross their path. Canon Maurice, Rector of Cottenham, organised sentries to watch from dusk until dawn from the top of the High Tower of Cottenham Church. [Canon Maurice was also intelligence officer, a task for which he was well trained, having served under 'Sapper' Col. M.C. McNeale, creator of Bull Dog Drummond, in World War One.] This observation post overlooked the fen to the north and to the east – country so well known to the TFB. Ralph Norman was often on watch armed with rifle, binoculars and a pint or two of beer.

In 1946 the TFB returned to their old established kennels in Barton where Major Barclay appointed Alan Baxter as master. He had come straight from the mastership of the Eton College Hunt and the TFB could count itself extremely lucky to have found a master with previous experience, for he had to contend with petrol rationing, flesh shortage, foot and mouth disease and terrible weather conditions. He also had to open up the country which had been neglected for four seasons, and in this he received the invaluable help of Mrs. Gingel, master of the Harriers, who did everything she could to see the TFB re-established. Alan Baxter recruited to his staff undergraduates who had returned from the war and most notably J.J. Kirkpatrick, who succeeded him as master in 1948. He is now Honorary Secretary of the Masters of Beagles and Harriers Association as well as Master of the Heythrop.

This post-forces generation proved one of outstanding administrators as well as huntsmen, as they were all trained organisers and leaders, capable of running the hunt efficiently and rebuilding goodwill with farmers. Having carried heavy responsibilities during the war, they found staff work with the TFB a much less exacting duty. Gradually the effects of the war disappeared. The pack was built up with great success, the hunting days were increased from two to three per week, and the annual visit to Northumberland was restored. On the social side the Interim Club, which had sought temporary accommodation in the Pickerel public house opposite Magdalene, was disbanded when the Pitt reopened. So that by the time Michael Parry carried the horn in 1968, and hunted the progeny of those Trinity hounds which had been so largely rescued by his father twenty-three years earlier, the martial days of the TFB had passed into history.

CHAPTER SIX

KENNELS AND KENNELMEN

It was R. Callaby, the dog fancier, who kenneled the first recorded pack of beagles in Cambridge. The hounds of R.G. Hoare's Foot Drag were housed, along with the ponies for the rowing coaches and a population of rats for the pit, in Callaby's yard in the enclosure known as Fort St. George. The venue changed when W.E. Currey brought his pack over from Ireland in 1867; he moved his hounds to the yard of the public house, known as the Merton Arms, in Northampton Street. Here the oft-changing pack remained from season to season fed on scraps from the Kitchens of Magdalene at 2s. a head. They were looked after by a kennelman, "Old Jackson", who had a reputation for immorality and resembled (and probably was) a retired bargee.

It is not surprising that when Rowland Hunt came up in 1880 he found the pack diseased, old and riotous. Hunt immediately looked round for a site for new kennels, and he soon acquired a vacant piece of land in Bermuda Road off the Histon Road. A subscription raised enough money to build new kennels and to buy a beagle cart, but not enough to buy the land itself, and this was purchased for £125 by the father of one of the whips, Mr. Pat Burgess.

The TFB remained in these kennels until 1930; during that period they bought a neighbouring plot of land for £100 as well as making considerable improvements to the yards. The main disadvantage was that there was no house for the kennel huntsman. Bob Floate senior, who was kennel huntsman for most of this period, lodged first in a house in the Histon Road and, later, in another adjacent to the kennels with a Mrs. Smith, who lived next to Crake's public house, the Prince of Wales. This was convenient as Bob could see the kennels from his window, but it also meant he was equidistant from Crake's pub, which often distracted his attention.

As the town of Cambridge expanded, so Bermuda Road became surrounded by new houses inhabited by people incapable of appreciating the sound of hounds in kennel. It was not long before the town council gave one month's notice for the TFB to quit. In 1930, the master, Bob Hoare, found temporary accommodation for hounds in some pigsties at Olders Farm on the Madingley Road, and the following year between July and October the present kennels were built on an isolated site about half a mile from the village of Barton.

Bob Floate, senior, in 1919.

Bob Floate, junior, in 1919.

The land, the kennels, the kennelman's house, the well and all the architect's fees cost only £2,000. Here, the TFB have remained, safe in the knowledge that they own the freehold and are far enough from the town of Cambridge to avoid any complaints from residents. In fact their closest neighbours are the ghosts in the graveyard opposite and John Hawkes of Haggis Farm; the latter has been a great friend and offered invaluable assistance to the TFB for many years.

Between the years 1883 and 1960 there were only two kennelmen and both were called Bob Floate. They were father and son and each served successive masters with loyalty and devotion. In so doing they established the good name of the TFB with the local tradesmen and provided yet another strand of continuity between one master and the next.

It was E.A. Milne who brought the first Bob Floate to Cambridge in 1883 to replace the notorious Jackson. Bob had previous experience of hounds, as his father had been part-time kennelman to the Storrington, and every morning before school, he and his brother had had to muck out kennels. He also had experience of knackery as he had served as a butcher's apprentice for a short period. This terminated after he rather unfortunately attacked the hated butcher with a carving knife, and he then pursued two equally short and equally disastrous careers as a gamekeeper and a plumber. At last he was discovered by E.A. Milne and introduced as kennelman to the TFB, which proved to be his vocation. His career is neatly summarised by F.C. Kempson:

> By birth a character, by trade a butcher, in default a bird scarer, and thence by desertion, kennelman to the TFB!

At first the terms of Bob's employment were extremely vague for he was taken on each year by a different master. In the summer of 1895, when the pack dispersed for the vacation, he was actually given notice with the option of returning at the beginning of the next hunting season. This rather unsatisfactory system ended with the creation of trustees in 1908. He was paid 18s. a week, excluding perquisites such as manure and bones. After the First World War, in recognition of the rise in the cost of living his wage was raised to £3 a week, plus 3d. for insurance for himself and his son. Mrs. Floate was also paid a small amount for washing the beagling breeches.

Bob and his family prospered. When not in kennel he was to be found in the Prince of Wales, where his brick red face and brilliant white moustache were a well known feature of the tap room. The hounds improved beyond recognition for he was an excellent kennelman, and immediately after the First World War he turned out a fit and workmanlike pack. H.A. Bryden inspected the pack in 1920 and had this comment to make:

On Sunday we had out the sixteen couples of hounds in kennel and had a good look at them all. I noted that two ten season bitches, Barbara and Bountiful, were still hunting as well as Gossamer (nine seasons), Juggler a capital stallion hound (eight seasons), and Gracious, Faithful and Jupiter (seven seasons) and that all were still working hard and going strong. This struck me as a fine tribute to Bob Floate the kennelman, who had been with the pack thirty-nine seasons.

Bob continued working until a few months before his death which occured on March 30th, 1927. His obituary in *Horse and Hound* ended with the words:

Thus passed away one who for 44 seasons did invaluable service to the hunt, and whose memory will never be forgotten.

It was a truly remarkable record and one which all ex-masters and masters should remember with gratitude.

Young Bob Floate immediately stepped into his father's shoes. Since the font he had been closely associated with the pack, because both he and his elder sister had been christened after Bob senior's favourite hounds. Young Bob received the names of Robert Foreman (Bob senior had originally wanted him christened Foreman Ferryman Floate, but the vicar disallowed it) and his sister received the names of Emelina Fretful. Although they were not twins both were christened at the same time for convenience sake. Emelina Fretful lived up to her name and had to be physically constrained during the ceremony for she had reached an age when she did not take kindly to the necessary acts of the ritual.

Young Bob served his apprenticeship under his father which, apart from menial tasks, involved walking out hounds with the masters and occasionally whipping-in. Before the season opened in October 1923, R.H. Studholme recorded in his diary "several days by myself with only little Bob to whip in."

Young Bob naturally continued his father's well tried methods of caring for hounds and throughout his long tenure as kennelman he turned out a number of Peterborough winners as well as conscientiously nursed the pack back to health after several attacks of distemper. Both he and his father were particularly interested in dosing, indeed when F.C. Kempson went to interview Bob Floate senior about his past history he found him "as a wind-up to the hunting season, dosing the entire pack with worm pills ..." One of young Bob's favourite mixtures was Pettifer's Green Oil sold by a man at Peterborough Hound Show who wore a grey bowler and gaiters.

Two causes of minor irritation to masters were Bob's taste for beer (inherited from his father) and his somewhat scruffy appearance. John

Representative of the third generation of the Floate family, photographed in 1937, coupled to a wise old hound with the TFB goat looking on.

Stourton (master 1952–53), who had been brought up in the beagling world by the immaculate Perkins at Eton, naturally found the comparison between the two kennel huntsmen more than striking. But Bob junior with his somewhat Irish manner was ideal for a university pack. He gave the undergraduates a completely free rein, he looked after the pack excellently and he was a well-known local man, trusted in and around Cambridge.

In 1962 young Bob became so ill that he could hardly lift up a hound. It was apparent that he would have to retire early and the master, Harry Wiggin, with his usual generosity, provided Bob with a cottage in Barton, where he lives to this day. Young Bob had many children most of whose godfathers were masters of the TFB and most of whom had spent their early years coupled to a particularly wise old hound who prevented them running on to the road. Unfortunately none of them showed the aptitude of their father or grandfather and the historic connection between the Floates and the Trinity Foot Beagles came to an end.

The two kennel huntsmen who followed the Floates both came from foxhunting backgrounds. The first was Tim Pearson. He started life in Yorkshire in racing stables, he then whipped-in to and hunted a number of foxhound packs including the South Bucks, the Woodland Pytchley, the Bicester, East Devon, the Hampshire Hunt and the Warwickshire. Although he learnt to control his voice when out beagling his allegiance always remained to foxhunting; all his instincts were those of a foxhunter; he believed it was vital to show sport at all costs; to lift hounds and lieu on to view.

Tim was an exceedingly tactful man, who perhaps more than any kennel huntsman to the TFB knew how to handle undergraduates. For the position of kennel huntsman to a university pack is entirely different to that to a school or forces pack. The university authorities play no part in the running or financing of the pack and the master is answerable only to the trustees. Under these conditions it is important for the kennel huntsman to get on with his employer who is many years younger than himself. The kennel huntsman should also be able to teach, and to point out to inexperienced masters their mistakes, without causing offence. This, Tim Pearson was able to do. He could converse on most academic subjects and would intersperse this erudition with flashes of hunting wisdom, as if to reinforce his argument. He would add weight for example to his views on neo-classical architecture with an observation such as: "Now 'eres a marvellous cart 'orse leg." Undergraduates rarely forgot the lessons taught during these supervisions. In 1967 he left the TFB to take up a position as Kennel Huntsman and Huntsman to the Clifton Foot Harriers where he remains to this day.

His successor, Jack Poile, had one of the longest entries in *Baily's Hunting Directory*. He started his foxhunting life as second horseman to the Eridge in

Tim Pearson, kennel huntsman from 1962 to 1967.

ʲack Poile, kennel huntsman from 1967 to 1976, photographed at a meet at Longstowe Hall in 1974.

1925, and went on to pursue a varied career serving with the West Tiverton, the South Dorset, the Tedworth, the Garth, the Llangibby, and the Romney Marsh. He ended his career with the Trinity Foot with whom he celebrated fifty years in hunt service.

Jack is remembered by most people for his strictures delivered to the master and whips as they disappeared almost faster than the hunted hare over the horizon. He tempered his anger, which was never deep rooted and never bitter, with a caustic wit, which was famous. On one occasion when the TFB were hunting at Alnham in Northumberland he turned to Robin Greenwood, who later became master, with the words: "Take a good look my boy, this is the nearest to heaven you will ever reach." And, although members of the field occasionally grew tired of him saying: "Run over there, will you, and see if that whipper-in is awake" (although one whipper-in, Ian Milligan, was actually caught asleep), his heart was always in the right place. He built up an excellent relationship with the farmers and turned out hounds beautifully. He was greatly supported by his wife, who always welcomed masters and whips. Sadly, both died within a short space of one another in 1977.

The present kennel huntsman is Jack Calder, who has served the TFB since 1976. He has done so with great success and it is hoped that he may carry on with the pack for many more seasons to come.

The running of the kennels has naturally always been the responsibility of the master and three large, leather-bound record books exist in which each master used to note down every detail of kennel management for the edification of his successor. These were last written up in the 1950s and each volume contains much entertaining information. There is a section on tradesmen in which S.J. Parsons, chemists of 405, Peas Hill, are recommended for worm balls and dressing; Redin of Trinity Street is recommended for all the printing; and R. MacKenzie of 59, Smithfield, London is recommended for kennel coats at 5s. each. And there are sections on insurance, distemper dressing and physicking.

The section on feeding remains particularly important as there is no regular supply of flesh from the arable farms around Cambridge, and it has always been necessary to go to a slaughterhouse for supplies. For most of the years covered by this history the supplier was a firm run by the Pink family. The original Mr. Pink lived on the Newmarket Road, who at the turn of the century used to supply horses at £1 each. His son moved to Earith and he continued to supply horseflesh to the TFB and he also walked puppies into the bargain. He died in 1939 and his son in turn took over the task of delivering the flesh (it cost 12s. 6d. a cwt.) in a horsedrawn cart to the kennels. This custom continued until 1952 when the third Mr. Pink retired. The pack now gets its flesh from a slaughterhouse on the outskirts of Cambridge.

With masters changing each season it is vitally important for the principles of hounds breeding to be passed down from one to the next. These were admirably laid down in 1920 by G.K. Dunning, who also noted that every hound that is eligible must be entered in the *Stud Book* by September 1st, and that each puppy be marked with a T and their litter number on the right ear. One of the main problems is organising puppy walkers. They are nearly always undergraduates who have to be approached in the Lent term. A number of farmers also walk puppies, most notably John Beaton of North Fen Farm, Rampton, who also offers the TFB generous hospitality during the season.

The puppy show is held in May or June. There has never been a shortage of experienced judges for this event as so many ex-masters are now masters of foxhounds. Apart from awarding silver spoons to the victorious walkers, G.K. Dunning also recommended: "Give a small prize to the groom or coachman or whoever looked after the winning puppy." A tent is provided by the Cambridge University Officers' Training Corps and all the leading farmers, walkers and subscribers are entertained.

In April and May when the puppies come in from their walks a carefully controlled system of exercise begins. This unfortunately has had to be curtailed in recent years due to the increase of motor traffic in and around Cambridge.

Each master aims to have his hounds fit before they go up to Northumberland in September, in the past the test of fitness was to go round the village of Madingley in under an hour. Often road exercising has led to some hair-raising encounters. Once whilst exercising along the Backs, Billy Whitbread stood helpless as he saw the entire pack hunt a cur up to the gate of Kings. They were only prevented from penetrating further by a don with a broomstick.

Other tasks recommended in the record books for the summer months were of a more ephemeral, if no less enjoyable nature, such as picking dandelion heads with Bob Floate to make wine for the farmers, or training puppies not to worry fowl with the aid of Billy Savidge's vicious Rhode Island Red.

All expenditure incurred in running the pack has to be met by the masters. And Michael Dill's cry which occurred half way through his mastership is a common one: "I am frankly frightened about the beagle finances." It is not surprising that John Stourton was greeted on a return visit with the words: "You are not *The* John Stourton, the only master who left a credit balance at the bank?"

The liquidity of the TFB depends upon income from subscriptions and fund raising events, such as profits from the Hunt Ball, the point-to-point and sweepstakes. Each master has been helped considerably by the manager of Barclays Bank, formerly Mortlake's, in Benet Street. The TFB have always banked there as one of their original trustees was a director. The relationship was cemented by the number of Barclays who hunted the pack and whipped-in. [At one time the connection between Barclays Bank and the beagling world was so strong that it was rumoured to become a director of the bank you first had to have been master of either the TFB or the Christchurch.] For many years the manager was a Mr. Steff, who deserves mention for the innumerable occasions he showed leniency and understanding towards temporarily impoverished masters.

If the master meets with seemingly insuperable problems then he knows he can always ask the advice of the trustees. The trustees play no active part in the running of the pack, but survey, like gods, the progress of each master from afar. The first trustees were appointed in 1908 when Mr. Parker of Mortlake's Bank and Dr. Rouse Ball, Fellow of Trinity paid off the debt of £108 for the site of the kennels, which was still owed to the trustees of Pat Burgess's father. Each year the masters paid back a small amount to repay this act of generosity. Before the First World War Mr. E.E. Barclay became a trustee. He and Mr. E.H. Parker looked after the pack throughout the duration, and they returned it to G.K. Dunning on the condition that the hounds remained the property of the trustees. Both the Parker and the Barclay families have continued to be trustees. Roger Parker, who whipped-in in 1910 and whose son whipped-in to John Leigh in 1956, lent continued support to the pack for many years. (He also happened to be a Director of Barclays Bank, Master of the Cambridgeshire Foxhounds for 25 years and Lord Lieutenant for Cambridgeshire.) In 1977 on the death of Bob Hoare, Charlie Barclay became Senior Trustee, following in the footsteps of his father and grandfather. Although the trustees do not have any funds at their disposal they are ultimately responsible for both the pack and the kennels, going some way to removing the burden of responsibility from the masters.

CHAPTER SEVEN

HOUNDS

An analysis of the bloodlines of the TFB is as complicated as delineating the relationship between masters. The pedigrees of the very early hounds do not exist, for it was not until Viscount Milton handed over the entire pack to his successor in trust that a consistent breeding policy was started. This has continued to the present day so that despite the disruption of two world wars the bloodlines of a number of hounds in kennel can still be traced, however tenuously, back to this period.

It is almost impossible to describe the earliest beagles that came to Cambridge. The Foot Drag were a scratch pack, with hounds brought from London, Kent or Oxford in the 1860s. They were probably very small hounds, only nine or ten inches high, which were still widely bred at that period. Descriptions of W.E. Currey's pack appear in the writings of F.C. Kempson. Currey brought them over from Ireland where the fashion for small beagles had never reached and the eighteen couple of hounds were on average over fifteen inches high; and Ernest St. Maur, who whipped-in, states that a number were black and tan. They remained in Cambridge until 1873 when the retiring master, H.C. Howard, took them down with him to hunt at his home in Cumberland. He set a precedent, followed for the next twenty years, whereby each retiring master sold to his successor only those hounds he did not want to keep. The new master then "topped up" the rump pack by buying in new hounds. Even Rowland Hunt, who aimed to breed for "nose, tongue, drive and perseverance", was guilty of depleting the pack in this way. In 1892 this convention was brought to an end by Viscount Milton whose action preserved the stock of hounds from one season to the next. Three years later a *Stud Book* was presented to the master by E.E. Barclay, and by 1903 the first TFB-bred dog hound was placed in the Appendix of the Stud Book of the Master of Beagles and Harrier Association. It was only a matter of time before the pack became fully registered.

There followed, under the experienced eyes of the Barclays of Brent Pelham and the loyal service of the Floates, a consistent breeding policy based on the lines of some of the TFB's most famous hounds. Continuity was maintained throughout the First World War as for half the duration the TFB were in

Cambridge and looked after by Major E.E. Barclay. He also presented G.K. Dunning in 1920 with beagles bought from Cranwell Air Base to supplement the existing TFB blood. The effect of the Second World War was much more serious; on the TFB's return to Cambridge, Major Birkbeck generously lent his pack to the master to hunt; and his stallion hounds provided a dramatic, but necessary, injection of new blood which weakened the traditional TFB lines. It was fortunate, therefore, that two other stallion hounds used at this time, United Cotswold Safeguard '44 and Eton College Woodman '45, both carried some of the most famous TFB blood in them providing a link between the earliest registered hounds and those of the present day.

After a period of eclipse, Roger Burton, master in 1976, revived the scientific breeding of hounds and made an attempt at bringing back more TFB blood from the old lines which had disappeared from the pack. This policy is being continued under the present regime and it is hoped that the TFB blood which may be traced in contemporary champions such as Eton Dipper, Wye Painter, Newcastle Viceroy, Dummer Woldsman and Ampleforth Admiral will be brought to good use.

The clearest and most interesting way to describe the various TFB pedigrees is to present a chronological "roll of honour" of hounds who represent different branches of the bloodline. A number of other hounds are also included who were not necessarily members of a TFB line or used for breeding purposes. They deserve mention for other, equally laudable, reasons which will become apparent.

BISMARK AND VICTOR

Described by Mr. Pat Burgess in 1880 as "an ugly coffin headed, but good, dog", Bismark was never taken home by a master and remained a stalwart of the pack for eight seasons. He is reputed to be the great grandsire of *Victor*, who was undoubtedly the best doghound in the 1890s.

Victor was by Mr. Johnson's Marvel and out of Countess, and he sired the whole of the 1896 and 1897 litters; he was also used as a stallion by other packs and was the great grandsire of Halstad Place Searcher '05. Evidence of a strong Northumbrian element at this period is reflected in the names of his puppies, which include Callaly and Reaveley. Most important of all he sired *Fretful*; the bitch after whom Bob Floate senior named his daughter and who was described by W.E. Paget as a "beautiful little hound built on Harrier lines". Her Dam was Fairmaid, who according to the same source was "amongst the best".

FOREMAN '05

Bred by G.B. Kidd in 1900 the first TFB dog after Victor to be registered in the *Stud Book*. Bob Floate junior was named after this famous hound and Foreman '05, along with Bismark and Victor represent the three patriarchs of the pack, who can be compared as a measure of their importance to the Hoare, the Buxton and the Barclay families. His dam was Fretful and his sire Chawston Guardsmen '00. Foreman is described by W.E. Paget as:

> A perfect topped hound with good shoulders well set on head and neck, wonderfully sprung ribs, good back and quarters and well carried stern. His top was hard to crab and the only fault I could find was his front, he was too broad and a little out at the elbows, but this I put down entirely to having entered him too young.

Godfrey Lawson, a whipper-in of this period qualifies this description.

> I think he was the finest looking doghound I have ever seen but he was rather apt not to throw his tongue sufficiently.

Foreman sired some of the best hounds in the pack immediately before the First World War and it is to him that all the most important TFB lines eventually ascend. His progeny included *General*, who was praised by Ralph Clarke in 1913 after a meet at Fulbourne for "hunting the fading line quite beautifully" and *Justice*, *Jollity* and *Rambler*, who were first at the kill after a hunt of one hour and ten minutes from a meet at the kennels during the same season.

MAGISTRATE '04
Out of Stoke Place Monitor '02, he was the TFB's first success at Peterborough as the best dog hound in 1904. He was continuously used for breeding.

DRUID '08
Out of Rambler, he came second in the stallion class at Peterborough in 1911. A leader of the pack, who coursed and killed a hare from Soham Mere in 1913.

JUGGLER '13
One of the most famous dog hounds ever bred by the TFB and considered to be the best representative of the "J" line. He was a great favourite of Bob Floate junior, who did not, however, name his own son after him. Along with Jupiter, Barbara and Bountiful, Faithful, Gossamer and Gracious, Juggler '13 formed the core of the pack during the First World War and carried on

The TFB parading at the Royal Show, Cambridge in 1960. (*From left to right*) Derek Smedley, Angus Armstrong, for many years the Northumberland secretary, Harry Wiggin, master, David Sinker, honorary secretary, and John Sclater, who succeeded as master in 1961. Young Bob Floate is in the background.

hunting afterwards into his tenth season. His great grandsire was Foreman '05, and he undoubtedly inherited the characteristic, as described in the *Stud Book*, namely "rather sparing in throwing his tongue, otherwise a masterpiece of his work" from Foreman. He was used a great deal in the early '20s and his kin include: *Diligent*, who won the first brood bitch class at Peterborough in 1921; *Draughtsman*, who won the second stallion hound at Peterborough in 1924 and who in turn was used extensively as a stallion, and *Dauntless*, sister of Draughtsman, who won the unentered bitches class and was reserve champion at Peterborough in 1920.

MAGISTRATE '22

His dam was Diligent and sire the noted Stoke Place Major '18. Described by A. Courtney Williams as:

> A dark tan-coloured dog, rather coarse in the coat, he stood slightly under fifteen inches. He was well balanced with a straight back and good shoulders, but need all the bone he had.

Bob Floate remembers him as being of foxhound-type in appearance, as well as being a splendid worker with a wonderful nose. He was greatly used by other packs and in particular by Major Birkbeck for whom he sired the outstanding hound Finder '31. He represents one of the most important TFB lines. His blood can be traced back to Foreman '05 and Halstad Place Searcher '05, and as grandsire of Croft Foreman '36 forward in two directions: via Dummer Woldsman '41, Eton Woodman '45 and TFB Serpent to the present "P" line of the pack; and via Eton Veteran '40, Newcastle Viceroy '49, Dummer Valient '53 and Sandhurst Vanguard '57 to the present TFB "V" line and young "W" line.

MAGISTRATE'S KIN

He was used surprisingly little within the TFB. Two puppies, Gameboy and Gambol, won the unentered couples class at Peterborough in 1928 and Gambol became Champion Brood Bitch in 1932. A different litter, Desperate, Destitute and Desolate, lived up to their names: Desperate died of distemper, Destitute got lost in Northumberland and Desolate only came third in the puppy show. Doctor, from the same litter, was used extensively in the 1930s.

RESTLESS '21

Described by Courtney Williams as "sandy tan in colouring, with very little white about her", she was a first class worker and her lines can be traced back to Foreman '05.

PIPER '25

Bred by Major Birkbeck and bought by the TFB in 1925. Described by J. Dimsdale as "a well made dog, perhaps a little light and narrow, but with depth". Used extensively for breeding in the 1920s and '30s. Was running up with the fast pack in his tenth season under Simon Lycett Green. One of Piper's best nicks was with *Dainty*, whose sire was Draughtsman.

HANNIBAL '28

Out of Hilda '22 (related to Foreman via Juggler) and Piper '25. Representative of the good mottled strain present in the pack in the early 1930s.

FOREMAN '33 AND FURY '33

Singled out by J. Dimsdale as two of the best working dogs.

SEARCHER '34

His sire was Doctor. He and his brother Solomon won the unentered couples at Peterborough in 1937 and he was Champion Dog Hound at Aldershot in 1938. He went on to breed a number of prizewinners, including Forager, Fallible and Fretful.

DRUMMER

Proof of the TFB moral that it is no good breeding to win on the flags if they cannot cross the plough. Drummer was Champion Dog at Aldershot in 1934 and was bought by J.J. Mann with great hopes. However, Mann wrote afterwards:

> If one had been a decent huntsman one would have shot him straight away, he was very fast and very independent and ran mute; all the worst qualities in a hound.

He was not used as a stallion hound.

MARCIA AND MADAM

Two black and tan bitches given to J.J. Mann by Lord Lonsdale. They were delivered to the TFB kennels in the famous yellow Rolls Royce.

GAMBLER '33

His sire was Doctor. Used occasionally as a stallion, but of greater use on he hunting field, where he could always be relied upon. At Scrainwood in Northumberland in 1937 he picked up the line against all odds, which resulted

United Cotswold Safeguard '44, from the painting by Michael Lyne. This hound was drafted to the TFB when Michael Lyne, ex-master of the United Cotswold, whipped-in to the TFB in 1944. In fact this hound was bred from the famous TFB "J" line through Trinity Jupiter '35.

in the death of the hare. J.J. Mann wrote in his diary: "Gambler really killed that hare, although he was nowhere near when we ran into her."

DEVIL '38

He was the angry young man of the 1930s, related through his dam Dairymaid to Draughtsman. Praised by all the masters who hunted him including Charlie Barclay and Michael Dill. Although ugly to look at he lived up to his name and was a great hare killer. On a day from Grange Farm in 1939 he killed a hare single handed. He survived the war and was used as a stallion both during and after it. Other hounds who formed the backbone of the pack in the late 1930s included: Fury, Barbara, Pitiful, Judith and Jaunty.

UNITED COTSWOLD SAFEGUARD '44

A stallion hound from the United Cotswold, Michael Lyne's pack, which joined the TFB for a period during the Second World War. Described by Courtney Williams as a fine worker and nicely formed, mostly white with light tan markings, and a little under sixteen inches in height. He belongs to the famous "J" line through Trinity Jupitter '35. He was used extensively by the TFB after the war, thus strengthening this line.

PROCTOR '45

His dam was Playful who was sound pre-war TFB stock, and his sire was Ampleforth Cromwell. Proctor won the stallion hound class in 1951; he is described as a bare fifteen inches who was short legged and well coupled. Both he and his brother Pirate had a trace of blue mottle. Proctor was used widely by other packs and bred a number of championship hounds. TFB winners by him included Chimer (reserve Champion) and his sister Cheerful (winner unentered class 1950). It was the Proctor and Pirate strain which provided the clutch of TFB winners at Harrogate in 1960 and 1961, namely Plunder and Prudence.

SAPPHIRE AND SERPENT '48

Two of the outstanding litter whose sire was Eton College Woodman '45 and their dam Sunshine, one of the pre-war TFB bitches. They were related on both sides to TFB Magistrate '22. Described by J.J. Kirkpatrick as perfect miniature foxhounds. Serpent is extremely influential in the main bitch line today, and bred Searcher by Pirate, winner of the couples class with Plunder at Peterborough in 1951. Sapphire won the brood bitch class in 1951.

PIPER '45

A bold little hound who tackled a hare single-handed and was bowled over in the process (in front of Lionel Edwards, who was sketching for a painting of the pack) at Cow Lane Rampton in 1950.

WINSOME '46
Pure bred pre-war TFB blood out of Devil and Wishful, considered by J.J. Kirkpatrick to be one of the best hounds in the pack.

THE PARK, KESWICK '66
Drafted in 1970, his sire was Beacon Kinsman '64. Related to many TFB lines by Major Birkbeck's Bluecap '31 and by United Cotswold Safeguard '44. He was used a great deal in the early 1970s.

VANISH AND VANITY '66
Two tan-coloured sisters used consistently with Park Keswick. Excellent in the field and related to Pirate '38 and Devil '38.

POSY '71
Was considered by the master, Mr. Duncan Hill, in 1978 to have the best nose in the present pack. She was out of Picture '64 by Park Keswick '66. *Welkin* '70, *Pilot* '71 and *Victor* '74 were considered the three other stalwarts of the pack in 1978. Great hopes are held for *Dalesman* '77, out of *Daphne* '69 and *Newcastle and District Valient* '72, these lines go straight back to Proctor '45.

CHAPTER EIGHT

NORTHUMBERLAND

Since the Second World War an increasing number of packs of beagles have made their way every September along the well-worn pilgrimage route to Northumberland, with the intention of hunting there before the season officially opens. Enthusiasts and hunting correspondents come from all over Britain to participate and to report, and the event has become known as the Beagling Festival. In 1977 apart from the TFB there were the Christchurch and Farley Hill, the Eton College Hunt, the Stowe Beagles, the Bolebroke, the Clifton Foot Harriers, the Purbeck and Bovington, the Derbyshire and Nottinghamshire, the Brighton and Storrington and the Airedale. It is often forgotten that the first pack of hounds to travel to Northumberland for this purpose was the Trinity Foot. They started doing so in the closing years of the 19th-century when there was a strong North country element in the TFB hierarchy, represented by the Carr-Ellison and Allgood families. Since then, the TFB have made the journey almost every year and on each occasion they never fail to delight in the best beagling country in Britain and to enjoy the boundless hospitality of its inhabitants.

The historic association between the pack and the county began when J.S. Carr-Ellison of Hedgeley went up to Trinity in 1886. His close friend and neighbour, A.M. Allgood of Ingram, was already an undergraduate and it was he who recommended beagling as a pastime to Carr-Ellison.

The first meet Carr-Ellison attended was at Quy and from that moment he became a devoted follower. In September of that year the two friends hunted their own scratch pack in the Cheviots and, having once sampled this heady experience, were keen to repeat it the following year when they augmented their pack with a few TFB puppies. By this time Carr-Ellison had been awarded his green coat and cap and had been offered the mastership the next season.

The first year the TFB hunted in Northumberland in earnest was 1888. The master took "ten couple of the best" north in September and kennelled them at Hedgeley. Bob Floate senior was in attendance and on first viewing the heights of Northumberland exclaimed "Lor Sir, these be wunnerful 'igh 'ills these be." It was a sentiment that has been shared by many a Trinity Foot

Oliver Larminie, master in 1975, hunting hounds in Northumberland.

Beagler since then as he has compared for the first time the steeps of Reaveley or Alwinton to the horizontal fen. It took Bob Floate senior some time to accustom himself to the ways of the Northumbrian hare, believing, until proved wrong, that if a hare ran into a sheep phanx all he had to do was close the gate behind it and trap it until the master and hounds caught up.

J.S. Carr-Ellison was an adventurous huntsman and believed in travelling right up into the hills, away from the tillage ground, before he began to draw. He transported his hounds, secured with pig netting, in a spring cart and would often travel all day to arrive at a suitable meet. Once driving to Byrness via Alwinton as dusk was falling, he almost ditched his cart and lost the pack on the line of a fox. An excellent day followed this mishap during which they killed their hare and surprised an escaped murderer who was so alarmed by the sight of the TFB that he was not apprehended until he was well over the Scottish border.

The appetites of Cambridge beaglers were whetted by the success of Carr-Ellison in Northumberland and it was under the auspices of his younger brother, George, that the visit by the TFB became an annual event. In 1895 George was offered a whip by K. Walker and that year persuaded the master to bring his hounds to Northumberland for the whole of the month of September. He was greatly supported in his arguments by R.F. Allgood who had been a whip for an unprecedented four seasons and whose elder brother had been the contemporary of J.S. Carr-Ellison. The Allgoods offered the remote farmhouse of Reaveley in the Breamish Valley for accommodation and kennelling, solving the one problem which might have made K. Walker hesitate in his decision.

The way was now clear for an expedition to Northumberland at the end of the summer vacation and, on August 31st, 1895, amidst great noise and excitement, a horsebox containing twenty couple of hounds, eight couple of puppies, one kennel man, one first whipper-in and one master of hounds was coupled to a train which left Bardsey Station at dawn, bound for Hedgeley. K. Walker described the journey in his hunting diary:

> Travelling in a horsebox is both extremely comfortable and without any of the usual problems that accompany travelling in a carriage designed for humans only. No-one can come in and one is shunted from one train to another without the trouble of changing. We breakfasted at York and lunched at "Canny Newcassel" and arrived at Hedgeley station on the Alnwick line at 2.30 p.m.

They were met by George Carr-Ellison who escorted them the three miles to Reaveley. There they soon settled in to the farmhouse, which they had to share with Mrs. Fenwick the house parlour-maid and cook, and her three cats, one cur, one spaniel, one fox terrier and a harrier pup. The hounds were kennelled in the yard and there was a puppy run in the coach house. The four weeks that followed were memorable; they beagled, cub hunted, shot partridge and rabbit, tickled trout and speared for eel, all under the most natural, not to say primitive, conditions.

Understandably, it was with great sadness that they left Northumberland for Cambridge, K. Walker wrote dismally:

> Back to Cambridge to hunt till term begins. Everything wrong, no food for the hounds, no water laid on, Bob's landlady away. Cambridge is depressing.

The TFB returned to Reaveley every year until 1912; an anonymous reporter in *Country Life* in 1926 recalled those days which seem to have remained unchanged from one season to the next.

> If living was cramped and rough − and one had to work for it − none of those who were fortunate enough to be invited will ever forget those joyous days and hilarious evenings, and above all the excellent sport.

In 1912 the farm was let to a tenant and in the following two seasons any thoughts of travelling to Northumberland were overshadowed by the threat of war. However the Allgood family remained closely associated with the pack throughout this period. In 1912 a cousin of G.H. Allgood whipped-in and his first cousin, I.A. Straker, was master in 1911. It is indeed fortunate for the TFB that the Allgoods went to Cambridge at all, for by tradition they had been an Oxford family and James Allgood, father of A.M. and R.F., had read divinity at Brasenose. There he distinguished himself at the end of a dinner after the Oxford University steeplechases by jumping the dining table of the White Hart Hotel, Aylesbury, mounted on a small grey horse from Simmonds livery stables. On going down from Oxford he became the parson of the village of Ingram, a living filled by his son a few years later. It is suggested by his granddaughter, Mrs. Church, who has always been a keen supporter of the TFB, that the reputation of her grandfather in Oxford militated against his sending his sons there and so they were sent to Cambridge instead.

It was not long after the end of the First World War that the TFB turned their thoughts towards Northumberland. In the summer of 1922 the master, W.H. Whitbread, and a pre-war Northumberland beagler, William de Geijar, made a reconnaissance trip north, staying with the Fenwicks at Long

Framlington. From there they visited all the farmers, landowners and masters of foxhounds and paved the way for the return of the pack to the county. The success of their venture relied upon finding a suitable alternative to Reaveley, for the farm was still let. Luckily they stumbled upon the ideal place which was to serve as a second home for the TFB for the next seventeen years; it was the Bridge of Aln Hotel. William de Geijar wrote some years later to the proprietor, Mr. Nicholas Beveridge, in terms which express the good fortune of their choice: "I for one can never be more grateful for all your kindness; it was indeed a lucky chance which brought me and Mr. Whitbread to the Bridge of Aln that summer's afternoon."

The Bridge of Aln Hotel is a large stone building situated on the Morpeth to Coldstream road. It was built in the 1880's beside the new railway line which ran from Cornhill to Alnwick and has changed little since then. The yard has extensive stabling and out-buildings, which originally sheltered the ponies and traps left there by the farmers from the West when they caught the train into Alnwick.

The hotel was so suited to the beaglers' needs that it could have been designed for that very purpose. The roomy stables provided ideal kennelling and Bob Floate and the kennel boy were put up in the bothy. The hotel itself had five bedrooms with eight beds in all, a dining room, a sitting room, a public bar, a select bar and one bathroom. The single drawback was not the solitary bath, but the fact that there was only sufficient water to fill it once a day. Each master took over the entire accommodation and outbuildings for the whole of September and the price for everything, including food, came to an invariable £135.

The key to the success of the Bridge of Aln Hotel was the proprietors, Mr. and Mrs. Nicholas Beveridge. Every year they showed the TFB wonderful hospitality, even by Northumbrian standards. And memories of beagling during these years are indelibly linked with them. The innumerable letters of gratitude preserved by the present Mr. Nicholas Beveridge, their son and owner of the hotel, are proof of this. None are more poignant than those written by disconsolate beaglers at the beginning of the War. Thomas Mann, serving with the Sussex Yeomanry in Hove, writes to them complaining of the "heat and overcrowding with children and refugees everywhere, which makes it a far cry from Whittingham", and William de Geijar, having joined the Observer Corps as a private, consoles himself "by trying to imagine I am spotting hares on Hartside instead of Junkers in the sky."

William de Geijar had been a mainstay of the Bridge of Aln every year between the wars. He kept in contact with the Beveridges throughout the rest of the year (he even sent them a copy of the first TFB history by F.C. Kempson for Christmas in 1934); and he provided extremely important continuity

Historic group of "heavies" in Northumberland, photographed at Hartside about 1935. (*From left to right*) J.C. Fenwick, K. Walker, H.G. Carr-Ellison, A.C. Lupton (*front*) and R.F, Allgood (*back*). Apart from J.C. Fenwick of Longframlington, who whipped-in to the TFB in 1865, the others in the group represent the full team of masters and whips who made the first organised expedition of Reaveley in 1895.

The 1937 group of undergraduates at the Bridge of Aln Hotel, Northumberland. (*From left to right*) Ian Anderson, Walter Scott, Peter Spens, master, Roger Channell, Maurice Allfrey. Bryce Knox seated at front.

between the successive masters and the Northumbrians. Even so, he appears to have been something of a mystery. He had gone up to Cambridge from Wellington in 1911 and went to Reaveley that year; and he left Cambridge with a First Class degree in history and immediately joined the expeditionary force to Mesopotamia. After the war, he worked for the League of Nations, but when this came to an end in 1921, apart from service during 1939–45, it appears that he was engaged in no obvious employment for the rest of his life. It was widely believed he was a member of the Secret Service. He also came out with the TFB once a term in Cambridge. The last time was in 1954, the year of his death.

The month soon flashed past: for the first fortnight they hunted every day except Sunday and in the second fortnight they hunted twice a day three times per week. The pressure of hunting led to the splitting of the pack either to a fast and slow pack or into dogs and bitches. On one occasion the entire pack united to hunt with the Guyzance beagles, almost as a prelude to the historic day on the outbreak of war in 1939. John Milburn and the TFB master, J.J. Mann, both carried a horn and whoever was nearest hunted hounds. They also managed to make use of the galaxy of sport available in Northumberland and crammed in days with the West Percy, the Bannamoor, the Percy and the Tyndale as well as fishing on the Aln and shooting. This superfluity of sport explains why hunting from the Bridge of Aln was considered unique. "It was ideal because you lived like a hound" explained J.J. Mann, "You were either hunting, which you were hopefully doing all the time, or eating or drinking or sleeping, that was all there was to do six days a week."

After the second world war the problems of taking the TFB to Northumberland seemed immense: during the war Mr. Beveridge had died and his widow no longer felt able to accommodate the TFB; petrol rationing was still in force and there was a nationwide scarcity of flesh. It was entirely due to Frank Goddard-Jackson, who had been master in 1927, that the pack returned so soon. Like Whitbread and de Geijar some twenty-eight years earlier he made an exploratory trip to Northumberland to see what chance existed for his old pack to return. Now that the Bridge of Aln was no longer available he lighted upon Rothbury as the most convenient centre for the TFB. There he arranged with Mr. Baker, the manager of the County Hotel, to put up the masters and whips and for Mr. Tulley, owner of the Railway Inn, to house Bob Floate and to kennel the hounds. He also organised scratch benches for hounds in the loose box and even an old army cooker and some coal to cook flesh. All was prepared for Alan Baxter to take them up in September when disaster struck; the pack went down with distemper and it was impossible to make the trip. Not to be daunted, Frank Goddard Jackson decided to make a "dummy run" with his own South Herts beagles, and had a most enjoyable fortnight regardless of a question asked in Parliament concerning his use of petrol on the journey north. He generously passed on all information resulting from the experience to the next TFB master, John Kirkpatrick, including, "Reaveley is a grand meet, there is an old TFB mask in the farm dated 1906."

Frank Goddard-Jackson had paved the way for the TFB's return in 1948. That season John Kirkpatrick, imitating his distinguished predecessor K. Walker, hired an entire railway wagon for the journey north equipped with sofas for the staff and stalls for the hounds. After so long an absence their presence was warmly welcomed by the farmers and landowners and it seemed a fitting start to a new era of Northumbrian hunting based on the town of Rothbury. The town has been described as a "clean old-fashioned town straggling at ease along the banks of the turbulent Coquet." The river has long been recognised as the best trout stream in Northumberland, and along its course there used to stand Rothbury race course where the famous "Heart of All England" trophy was run. The TFB have inhabited two of its hotels, the County and the Coquet Vale. The County was managed by Mr. Baker, who although not a sporting man, loved a party with the TFB regardless of his other guests. Unfortunately in 1960 it became an old peoples home and thus an inappropriate place for the TFB to remain and they moved to the Coquet Vale where the Richardsons acted as tolerant hosts to the often quite extraordinary behaviour of members of the hunt. One of whom once fell out of an upper room onto the ground below only to arise unscathed from the experience. Hounds were kennelled in the Station Hotel and the cats and cur dogs would receive a regular pasting from the pack whilst exercising on Sundays. In 1967 the Milburns of Gillheuch kindly offered the use of their stables to the TFB which they accepted.

Unfortunately, Rothbury developed as an increasingly popular tourist centre and by 1975 the Coquet Vale had become too expensive for beaglers; it was also regularly filled with coach parties who were not sympathetic to undergraduate noise and riot. The TFB moved its centre for the fourth time; kennelling the hounds in the old Northern Counties Otter Hounds kennels near Callaly Castle and housing the masters and whips in the Queen's Head, Glanton. When Major Browne generously give permission to the Trinity Foot to kennel their hounds at Callaly High Houses as they are called, he renewed an association between the castle and the pack which had begun with K. Walker's first visit in 1888. Then Callaly was one of the original meets of the TFB and the hounds were kennelled the night before in the same kennels that they use now. K. Walker set off at five in the morning to get to the meet on time; unfortunately the day that dawned was very hot and there was very little scent.

Wartime beagling at Low Reith, Durham in 1945. From the painting by Michael Lyne, who whipped-in to John Parry seen here running behind the pack.

The TFB have opened up new country in Northumberland each time they have changed their habitation, but the core of the country, first hunted by H.S. Carr-Ellison in 1888 has remained the same. This is the area that has the Morpeth/Coldstream Road as the Eastern boundary and the River Coquet as the Southern boundary. The meets of Harbottle, Alwinton, Biddlestone and Elilaw determine the boundary to the West and to the North. It is worth digressing with a short history of the packs of Northumbrian hounds, which have hunted this area, as many of the local families who ran them have naturally had long association with the TFB. In the early 19th-century this territory was part of the far-flung Northumberland and Berwickshire Hunt, although a number of small packs, most notably the Tossom Foxhounds and Rev. James Allgood's Harriers hunted within it. When H.S. Carr-Ellison first hunted here in 1888 it formed part of W.C. Selby's Biddlestone Country, and in fact H.S. Carr-Ellison later whipped-in to him. In 1892 Major A.H. Browne hunted the country for one season with the Callaly Hounds and then from 1893–1917 it became the Coquetdale, which for varying periods had Mr. T.C. Fenwick-Clennel, Mr. L. Fenwick and Mr. Basil Hoare as masters. In 1919 the pack was restarted by Major Alex Browne as the West Percy.

Today the TFB hunt almost entirely in this country, and they are deeply grateful to the two joint masters of the West Percy, Sir Ralph Carr-Ellison and Sir John Milburn, for granting them permission to do so. Both masters have strong links with the TFB. Sir Ralph Carr-Ellison is son of J.C. Carr-Ellison, and Sir John Milburn was master of the TFB in 1939. The country is also part of that belonging to the Newcastle and District Beagles, and over many years the masters, Colonel J.R.N. Bell and Colonel L.Y. Gibson have graciously extended their permission to the TFB to hunt it. For this favour the TFB are ever in their debt.

This stretch of country has resulted in some of the best hunts in a master's life-time and diaries are full of superlatives referring to them. Of Reaveley, John Sclater wrote when Jeremy Ventham was hunting hounds, "The views of Reaveley are so wonderful that it is impossible not to enjoy oneself thoroughly. The young entry seem to be doing well." Of Alnham when John Kirkpatrick was hunting hounds Pat Lloyd, his secretary, wrote "an especially memorable day when hounds ran unaided over a grand line of moorland country, worked painstakingly through a large bracken brake and finally killed their hare in the open after a hunt of sixty-five minutes"; and of Alwinton described by J.D. Ridell in 1923 as "one of the best days hunting I can remember."

When K. Walker brought the TFB to Northumberland in 1895 he initiated the most famous meet of the TFB, at Long Framlington. It was by invitation of Dr. J.C.J. Fenwick, who was one of the pioneers of beagling in Cambridge, having whipped-in to H.W. Bagnall in 1865. From the very first the meet at Long Framlington proved a success. Hounds and staff spent the previous night at the hall and as a result awoke at 5.30 "feeling rather cigar and whiskyfied." They met at seven, mounted, and enjoyed a grand hunt after a jack hare, killing in the open. K. Walker wrote in his diary:

> Screaming scent breast high. Hounds flew, Gambler leading them, with Gaudy and Garnish close behind ... Took hounds home to Reaveley via Bridge of Aln ... Never were such hounds, such horses, such men.

A succession of memorable hunts followed. Typical is the one enjoyed by Bob Hoare in 1930; somehow they managed to have three good hunts in a gale as well as cope with the surfeit of hares which is always a problem.

> Hounds hunted their first hare halfway up Mount Pleasant and back, when they changed to a fresh one. They then put up a really good performance hunting for some forty minutes in a gale before running into her at the kiln. A third hare skirted Mount Pleasant but after about forty minutes ran straight up to Long Framlington chapel. From there she went about two fields, when hounds ran from her scent to view and bowled her over in the open.

Throughout the 1920s and 1930s they used to stay the night before at the house with the hounds in the stables and Bob in the village. May Fenwick remembers that it was complete chaos with no-one getting a wink of sleep all night. She, with her two sisters, used to ride out beagling; it proved an excellent means of getting one's horse fit for hunting as well as for viewing the hare, particularly if it went over the hill at Cragside.

Often there would be as many as seven Miss Fenwicks out with the TFB for their four cousins from Brinkburn Priory were keen supporters, and they arranged a new meet at their home, Brinkburn Hope, after the First World War. Their hospitality certainly proved consolation to the TFB after a dreadful day experienced by Jock Mann in the bracken because "the day did not end on a sad note for at Brinkburn Priory one of Mrs. Fenwick's most excellent luncheons awaited us."

When the TFB moved to the Bridge of Aln, meets on the other side of the Wooler-Morpeth road were initiated. These included Titlington, Leamington, Bolton and the Bridge of Aln itself. The move to Rothbury extended their country to embrace Harbottle by invitation of the Fenwick-Clennel family (this resulted in a red-letter day for Michael Parry); and Rothbury itself where

John Sclater killed three hares in the first hour. Distant meets have also been added to the card; such as Mindrum the home of Perry Fairfax on the Scottish border and Tarset the home of Matthew Festing.

To keep in touch with the farmers and landowners there exists a *Northumberland Book*, similar to *The Farmers' Book*. In the past the masters have been greatly assisted in the updating of the information contained in this book by the services of Dr. Angus Armstrong who acted as unofficial secretary to the TFB in Northumberland. He whipped-in to Harry Wiggin in 1959, but his links with the pack run deeper than that for he is the nephew of the Misses Fenwick of Long Framlington. No man was better equipped to provide information on the changes within the farming community for he is, like his forebears, the doctor of Rothbury. Since 1977 Matthew Festing, a native of Northumberland and master of the TFB in 1969, has taken on much of this work, thus greatly contributing to the success of each visit.

The two hazards of beagling in Northumberland are the lack of scent and the bracken. J.J. Mann describes a typical day from Hartside which illustrates both these points:

> The fast pack. Another grilling day ... hare went down the road and slam over Reaveley Hill. I managed to pick the wrong route and found myself in six foot of bracken. I could make nothing of it ... I have never found worse going what with the bracken and shale screes, the south side of the hill was so hot that the scent would not lie because I viewed the hare just two minutes in front of hounds and they would hardly own it ... Blew off and Mrs. Bryant from Ingram gave us refreshments, I drank about three pints and had a vast quantity of ginger cake ... (On the way home) Just before the bridge at the bottom we found Bob had been watching our hare ... Took hounds out of trailer and went straight to top of hill. This hunt lasted another hour and I stopped hunting at 2.10.

As the report in *Horse and Hound* ruefully comments: "So much for the dead beaten hare."

The following week the master tried to overcome these hazards by hunting at Glanton Pike at night. Unfortunately the experiment was abandoned because of fears of disturbing stock.

Hunting in Northumberland for the first time can prove an extremely daunting experience for a young huntsman. Not only is he faced with a strange country, but also by an intimidating array of followers. For once a TFB master has hunted hounds in Northumberland he reserves the right to return any September and join the "heavy brigade" on the hilltops. Its members vary from generation to generation but throughout the 1920s and 1930s they consisted of the original TFB Northumbrian beaglers: namely J.S. Carr-Ellison and his brother George, Cis Lupton, A.M. Allgood, Dr. J.C.R. Fenwick and K. Walker. The latter, who was by now master of the Pembrokeshire, dominated the skyline proffering misleading information to the master. He had worn a monocle since his Cambridge days, but it had no effect upon his myopia. When Frank Goddard Jackson was hunting in 1927 K. ordered "brother Nigel" to go and enquire if a yokel had seen the hare. Nigel, who had been master in 1897, replied that it was not a yokel but a scarecrow. "Never mind" said K. the senior master to the last, "if I tell you to go and enquire, go and enquire". Luckily K. was not only generous with his advice but also with his hospitality. He used to stay at the Red Lion, Glanton, and gave dinners for the TFB to which he asked all the local girls such as the Misses Fenwick and the Misses Allgood. He also gave picnics after meets. Brandon Cadbury, after a meet at Glanton, had "an excellent lunch with K. Walker, finishing with kummel and cigars."

It was not long before Frank Goddard-Jackson himself rose to the ranks of the brigade and he still follows regularly. Another supporter from a slightly earlier undergraduate generation is Albert Kirkup; he whipped-in to A.L. Barclay in 1924 and now comes out as a mounted follower. There are no barriers of age to the hill top supporters: Paul Clarke, who whipped-in in the early 1960s, is a member and so is Matthew Festing, master as recently as 1971. His immediate successor, Tom Ramsden, witnessed the full weight of his experience brought to bear on a typical problem posed by hunting in Northumberland.

> On Saturday, we met at Green Leighton. There was little scent and most of the day was spent in a field with long grass out of which the hares refused to run. Hounds killed one leveret and then found an older hare which from time to time abandoned the long grass and made a short circuit on the lower ground. During one of these excursions two hares approached a wall on which members of the field were sitting. One hare turned right handed and the other turned left. When hounds appeared a heated debate was already in progress as to which was the hunted hare. One of the ex-joint masters, forgetting he was not on the parade ground, voiced his opinion with shouts of rubbish, as some member of the field disagreed with him. Hounds eventually killed their hare under a gate near the farm.

A calming influence on such scenes is the approach of the spatted figure of Monsignor A.N. Gilbey. Although a devoted supporter of the TFB in

Cambridge he had never been to Northumberland until William de Geijar introduced him to the custom in 1949. He stayed at the County Hotel and when that closed he moved to the Three Wheat Ears at Thropton. There he is admirably looked after and he in turn looks after the spiritual needs of the community by celebrating Mass every morning at 7.30. The Catholic church is only a short distance from the Inn, but it still entails a certain rush in the mornings and necessitates the wearing of beagling breeches under his cassock. There is just time for a quick breakfast before the meet at 9.0 a.m. realising the description found in the medieaval romance of Sir Gawain and the Green Knight of "mass in the mornynge and hunting all daye."

With so many supporters and friends, every evening is soon filled up with some form of entertainment. Over the years the families of Fenwick-Clennell, Armstrong, Milburn, Carr-Ellison, Burrow, Sordy, Buckle, Lidell, Ravensworth and Fenwick have made Northumbrian hospitality famous, and during the 1960s the TFB tried to repay their debt by organising a small hunt dance in return. Often, of course, such jollity can have adverse effects upon members of the hunt staff the following day. After one particularly good dinner the meet was at Guyzance and one of Michael Sclater's whips was doing his best at making polite conversation to the late Lady Milburn until he could control himself no longer and was violently ill at her feet. Lady Milburn with a look of profound sympathy, patted him gently on the head and said: "Poor boy, poor boy, I know exactly what it is like."

Of all reasons why Northumberland has appealed to the TFB, the most important must be its remoteness. To beagle in Northumberland is to be transported into another world where the hares are bigger and stronger, where hounds seem to fly and not just to run, and where the inhabitants welcome the TFB as if it were a homecoming; in short where hunting is life and the country appears to be designed for this very purpose.

CHAPTER NINE

MODERN BEAGLING

The most striking aspect of the Trinity Beagler is that he changes little from generation to generation. His vim and enthusiasm remain alive regardless of contemporary puritan attitudes towards his way of life. Two of the most recent masters, Ted Foster (1977) and Duncan Hill (1978), both provided excellent sport and the effervescence of their social activities was almost unparallelled. Ted Foster's final beagle dinner of the Lent term had to be held in Paris, as no British town, least of all Cambridge were prepared to act as hosts to the high spirited members of the Beagle Club. During Duncan Hill's mastership the Edwardian tradition of holding dinners in members' rooms was revived. Both masters come from Shropshire and over the Christmas vacations of 1977 and 1978 they renewed the association between the TFB and this county, which had been formed in 1880 by Rowland Hunt, when they took hounds home to hunt. It is hoped that both masters will continue to follow Rowland Hunt's example and become masters of the Wheatland.

The TFB is at present in the capable hands of Charles Smyth-Osbourne MH and Henry Fayre MH. Charles Smyth-Osbourne is late master of the Eton College Hunt, and whilst at Eton gained notoriety by hollering a hare on South Meadow, whilst being forced to play the Field Game on a hunting day. The visit to Northumberland continues as do all the other traditions described in this book. All that remains is to wish them every success during their mastership, and good luck to those who follow in their footsteps.

The author as master in 1973.

APPENDIX I

THE BEAGLE SONG

The beagle song was composed by H. S. Gladstone in 1897 at the request of the master, G.D. Hall, who, according to the composer, wanted to sing it during the vacation. It was written to be sung to the tune of the Meynell Hunt. Messrs Redin & Co published it in pamphlet form and it was sold at 6d. a copy. It enjoyed considerable success at the time of publication and it runs as follows:

Of all national sports
Of all manner of sorts,
There is one which must stand quite alone;
You may talk of a chase,
Or of rowing a race,
But beagling will e'er hold its own,
And I'll vow that the Trinity Pack
Can never be thought to be slack,
When the men at its head
Are the best ever bred
At getting hounds back on the track.

Chorus (please).
Then Hurray for the Trinity Beagles
They're as swift and as clever as eagles;
And a man must run hard
If he'd not be debarred
Seeing Pussy rolled o'er by the Beagles.

Oh! well I recall
Those grand days at the Hall,
When we gaily set off in a thaw,
Down some crowded small street,
To a far-distant meet,
Where we straightway proceeded to draw.

Just think of the fine hunting morn
And the merry toot, toot, of the horn,
With a loud "Tally-Ho!"
As we see the hare go
From the field which the hounds haven't drawn.

Chorus

We shall have to go fast
(If we hate to be last)
For "Pussy's" a clinker today;
Look! There she goes now,
By the edge of the plough,
While the hounds are quite three fields away.
There's a check! Well they won't stop for long!
Look there they are off again strong!
For close to that gate
They hit it off straight,
Its seldom that Walker casts wrong.

Chorus

It's the deuce of a run,
And I'm pretty well done,
But "Puss" can't be far off her death;
It's lucky by gad!
For I think every lad
Has pretty well used up his breath.
Why, now, in that field on the right,
One can see a most glorious sight:
Hounds are in the same field,
And poor Pussy must yield,
And our pups shall be blooded tonight!

Chorus

Oh! Haste to that yell,
Which is Pussy's death-knell,
Ee'r the hounds begin breaking her up;
When the trophies are got
We soon give the whole lot

To the pack — and a bit to each pup.
Well there! It has been my endeavour
To show that our beagles are clever.
And I think that the most
Of you'll join in the toast
Of "The Trinity Beagles for ever!"

Chorus.

APPENDIX II

THE CAMBRIDGE UNIVERSITY DRAG HOUNDS

Tracing the history of the Drag is bedevilled by the fact that most of the records were burnt in 1939, and any that might have survived the holocaust have since been lost. The chance discovery of a pamphlet in the possession of Mr. Philip Sinker, a trustee of the Drag, written by B.G.E. Webster in 1955, has resulted in much of the information given below.

Drag hunting must have been organised on an informal basis in Cambridge as early as the 1840s as the description quoted in Chapter One reveals. The story of the bewildered North American, who sampled the extremely dangerous and violent delights of drag hunting, was quoted from *Sketches of Cantabs* by "John Smith" which was published in 1849 several years after the author went, or had been sent, down.

The first day of the official drag hounds in Cambridge is mentioned in a letter in F.C. Kempson's *History of the Trinity Foot Beagles*. The letter is written by Charles Hoare, whose uncle had brought the beagles to Cambridge in 1863. In it he refers to the Drag as having been started by Harcourt Vernon and A.C. Barclay. The first hounds were fetched from Bishops Stortford in a cab, and their first run was over Cottenham Pastures. Characteristically the day ended with "a lively dinner" in Magdalene. No date is given for this first line, but it must have been before 1855, which is the date mentioned in Baily's as the year of the founding of the Drag. The two masters, wrongly named as the founders, were Mr. Mortimer and Mr. Digby Caley. It is from their mastership that there has been a practically unbroken line of succession.

The earliest kennels were at Brick Fields near Trumpington, but these were soon moved to Newnham Croft, for the convenience of the admirable kennel huntsman called Leete. He was a failed farmer but his popularity with the farming community led to many lines being opened up for the undergraduates. Undoubtedly he contributed greatly to the roaring success of the drag in the late 19th century. J.M. Paulton writing in *The Badminton Magazine* in 1878 described his technique as follows:

> Leete was a worthy old fellow, but he always looked more than anything like a bombaillif out for a holiday. He rode an old three-

legged horse, rather more shaggy if possible than himself, both of them diffusing a constant and overpowering odour of aniseed. You could always "wind" Leete across the road or round the corner. How in the world he managed to lay the drag as he did, and to negotiate the obstacles over, through and under which he and his old horse crawled was a matter of amazement to us all. When he came to a stiff place he would dismount, throw over one end of the line to which was attached the rabbit skin that carried scent, and if he could not get over or through would ride round by some gate. If as occasionally happened he had not taken sufficient start or the drag was extra fast, we would run him to view a fence or two from home, and then it was a sight for gods and men to see him finish in front of hounds.

Leete died in service in 1884 after 29 years with the drag. His son H. Leete immediately took over, and he was still active as the kennel huntsman in 1909.

One of the most dashing periods of the Drag history were in the 1870s and 1880s when the sons of the aristocracy and upper classes raced at break-neck speed over monstrous fences in pursuit of Leete and his drag. These days are wonderfully evoked by Sir Alfred Pease, whose two books *Half a Century of Sport* and *Hunting Reminiscences* contain descriptions of the Drag when he was master in 1878. Pease describes his runs with the Drag as though they were a race. For example he noted at the end of the Over Drag that he saw the leaders, Lord Binning, Jimmie Orr-Ewing and Algy Lawley, later the Rev Lord Wenlock, charge the last fence:

> It was a strong dense bullfinch and all fell into the finishing field. Seeing all this grief from the rear I came over the gate and won the Drag.

Lord Binning on his famous horse Mosquito accomplished some extraordinary feats out drag hunting, on one occasion Pease saw him take two closed railway gates, as a train was approaching, on the high road in the Waterbeach Drag. It is no wonder that Pease wrote:

> Of all horses under the sun an undergraduate's horse is the most wonderful. I have known Philips [with whom he shared lodgings] ride with the drag on Friday, hunt with the Fitzwilliam on Saturday, again on Monday, and go to the Pytchley (Woodland) on Tuesday, Lucifer (appropriate name) his mount each day.

By the 1890s the Drag was not in such a flourishing condition, the reason being, according to the master, J.F. Ramsden, "the increasing popularity of rowing particularly amongst old Etonians." No doubt to improve the image of the Drag, J.F. Ramsden started to hunt a carted stag, which he bought from Porter of Thames Ditton for £12. Support noticeably improved although the habit of the hind of circling the field twice and often jumping out of the gate over which she had entered, was often disconcerting for the amateur huntsman. The tradition of hunting a stag in this way was continued until 1909 when the RSPCA brought a court case against the master for trying to persuade a reluctant hind to leave the gatekeeper's yard at Great Shelford Crossing.

From that date the pack returned to hunting a conventional drag. After the Second World War the prospects of the Drag did not look particularly hopeful, but thanks to the energy of Nat Sherwood who became the master and Mr. Peter Grain, they soon found kennels and collected a pack together. The pack is now kenneled with the TFB on the Barton Road and they offer an extremely full and varied card, which their late Victorian forebears would be proud of.

APPENDIX III

THE WHIP CLUB

The Cambridge University Whip Club was founded in 1938 by Gilbert Monckton, on the disbanding of his Number 4 Troop, Cambridge University Cavalry Squadron (more familiarly known as Monckton's Horse). Twenty-two rules of the Club were drawn up the most important being:

> That the object of the club be to encourage the sport and art of driving, and to further the more general use of the horse.

Its inception was announced in a letter to *Horse and Hound* written by Gilbert Monckton:

> Sir, In view of the recent correspondence on driving it might interest your readers to know that a club has recently been formed at Cambridge with the object of encouraging the sport and art of driving. It is proposed to hold meetings regularly throughout the term. At present membership is small, but we hope for a more general interest after the opening meet of the term on Nov 3rd.

For the opening meet the club assembled in New Square and drove out to the Cambridgeshire Harriers point-to-point at Cottenham. The precedent of meeting on a race day was continued and numerous meets were arranged followed by drives either to Cottenham or Newmarket. The club caused a considerable stir wherever it went and frequent mention was made to it by the press. In 1939 *Varsity* reported them at the C.U.U.H.C. point-to-point:

> In spite of a bitter East wind and hint of rain in the air, the first day's racing drew a good attendance, including nearly 30 members of the newly formed whip club, who arrived in a varied assortment of horsedrawn vehicles, all wearing their regulation green coats and 'ats ... this year there were considerably fewer falls than usual ... the hunters challenge cup was a procession more than a race ... The

Athanaeum Challenge cup was a poor race only redeemed by Mr Colin MacAndrew's fine riding.

[Colin MacAndrew, a member of the Whip Club, later became a famous amateur huntsman.]

If there was no race meeting then an excursion around Cambridge was arranged, often with an expert giving a talk on the art of driving, after lunch. In 1940 Michael Dill, who had become secretary to the club records in his diary:

> The drive out via Fen Ditton is one of the most delightful within a short distance of Cambridge. Shortly after we reached the Bridge Hotel, Clayhythe Major Faudel-Phillips arrived. After an enjoyable meal by the riverside, Major F.P. rigged up some reins on the teatable and gave us excellent instruction in the elements of the cart. He then sped us on our way with some calls on the horn.

During the summer term the club found other diversions. They attended the May Bumps for example, and again their presence received comment from the press. *The Sunday Times*, reported that Jesus (true to form) remained head of the river for the fifth year running and that:

> ... the Mays finished in a blaze of glory at Cambridge this evening, when both banks of the river were crowded with spectators. The various enclosures were well patronised and members of the University Whip Club drove down by road in a variety of ancient horse-drawn vehicles.

The club also patronised the Beagle cricket match that summer lunching first at the Three Horse Shoes. And on the 739th Proclamation of Reach Fair on Rogation Monday they offered to drive the Lord Mayor of Cambridge to the event in his state coach, which was on exhibition in the museum. The mayor, somewhat unimaginatively, refused.

To complement the daytime activities, dinners were instituted. The first was held on November 24th, 1938 and consisted of seven courses. And at each succeeding dinner they conformed to the rule 18 of the club which was:

> At each dinner the following toasts be drunk. The King, secondly the Whip Club, thirdly the Horse coupled with the Road and lastly Mr Harry Stevenson, Cambridge Graduate and "The Wonder of the Age".

Mr. Harry Stevenson was honoured in this way because on going down from Trinity College, Cambridge about 1825 he caused a stir in society by turning his hobby of driving a stage coach into a profession. His coach was called "The Age" and it ran from the Bull and Mouth, Regent Circus to the fashionable resort of Brighton. It was noted at the time that "amidst all the profaneness of the calling he preserved the character of a gentleman". This maintenance of standards which led to liveried servants accompanying the coach, and to the offering of sandwiches and sherry to the passengers undoubtedly was the cause of his financial ruin. Poor Stevenson died young but before doing so uttered some memorable last words. When his death drew near he asked those around to lift him up in bed, so that he sat as though on the box of his coach, then grasping imaginary reins in his hands he cried "Let them go George, I've got 'em". He then fell back and expired.

Harry Stevenson was the absent patron of the club and the President was Sir Arthur Quiller Couch, better known as "Q", who found time from compiling the Oxford Book of English Verse to attend both drives and dinners. He is still remembered by many people in Cottenham who saw him being driven to the point-to-points and the beagle cricket match, immaculately dressed, with a dark red carnation in his buttonhole. Although the President remained in Cambridge throughout the War; and all the Whip Club relics including a portrait of Harry Stevenson, were safely housed in the Interim Club; with the departure of Michael Dill from Cambridge in 1940 the short, but glorious life of the Whip Club came to an end.

APPENDIX IV

LIST OF MASTERS

I THE FOOT DRAG

1862–6   (1) R.G. Hoare
          (2) Courtney Tracey
          (3) H.H. Bagnall

II THE "FOOT BEAGLES"

1867–70   W.E. Currey, M.A.

III THE TFB

1870–1	W.H. Rodwell
1871–2	H.C. Howard
1872–3	H.C. Howard
1873–4	G.H. Longman
1874–5	V.W. Vickers
1875–6	V.W. Vickers
1876–7	V.W. Vickers
1877–8	W. Cunliffe
1878–9	C.A. Tennant
1879–80	C.A. Tennant
1880–1	R. Hunt
1881–2	R. Hunt
1882–3	W. Watkin Wynn
1883–4	E.A. Milne
1884–5	E.A. Milne
1885–6	C.F. Young
1886–7	A.F. Pease
1887–8	A.F. Pease
1888–9	J.C. Carr-Ellison
1889–90	A.C. Hall

1890–1	A.C. Hall
October 1891	P. Conolly
January 1892	Viscount Milton
October 1892	R.S. Hicks
January 1893	W.E. Rogerson
1893–4	E.R.T. Corbett
October 1894	E.R.T. Corbett
January 1895	(Committee)
	K. Walker
1895–6	K. Walker
October 1896	C.H.D. Tanqueray
January 1897	N.O. Walker
October 1897	N.O. Walker
January 1898	C.F. Mitford
October 1898	C.F. Mitford
Committee dissolved	
January 1899	H.S. Gladstone
1899–1900	C.B. Kidd
1900–1	W.E. Paget
October 1901	W.E. Paget
January 1902	H.G. Barclay
October 1902	D.G. Hoare
January 1903	D.G. Hoare
1903–4	A. Buxton
1904–5	C.G. Hoare
1905–6	C.R.H. Wiggin
1906–7	M.E. Barclay
1907–8	M.E. Barclay
1908–9	A.G. Murray Smith
1909–10	W.H. Wiggin
1910–11	T. Holland-Hibbert
1911–12	L.A. Straker
1912–13	G.W. Barclay
1913–14	R.S. Clarke
1914–21	G.K. Dunning
1921–23	W.H. Whitbread
1923–24	R.H. Studholme
1924–5	A.L. Barclay
1925–26	R.C. Parker
1926–27	A.F. Goddard-Jackson

1927–28	J. Abel-Smith
1928–29	W.W. Hicks Beach
1929–30	P.W. Paget
1930–31	R. Hoare
1931–32	W.J. Stirling
1932–33	T.F. Dimsdale
1933–4	S.E. Lycett Green
1934–5	J. Dimsdale
1935–6	B. Cadbury
1936–7	J.J. Mann
1937–8	W.P. Spense
1939	J.N. Milburn
	C.G.E. Barclay
	J.M.G. Dill
1940	J.M.G. Dill
1940	J. Holland-Hibbert
1944–6	J. Parry
1946–48	A.G.L. Baxter
1948–50	J.J. Karkpatrick
1950–51	J.J. Buxton
1951–52	R.L. Hancock
1952–3	J.R. Stourton
1953–4	J.D. Alliot
1954–5	S. Cresswell
1955–6	J.R. Leigh
1956–7	P.J. Hartington
	P.A. Alliot
1957–8	S.E. Scrope
	C.H.A. Bott
1958–9	T.E.B. Hill
1959–60	J.R. Stevens
1959–61	H.W. Wiggin
1960–61	J.R. Sclater
1961–62	J.R. Sclater
	C.F.H. Morland
1962–3	H.J. Scrope
	J.R.O. Collin
1963–4	J.R.O. Collin
	J.J.R. Pope
1964–5	J.J.R. Pope
	J.J. Ventham

1965–6	J.J. Ventham
	M.V. Sclater
1966–7	M.V. Sclater
	P.N.W. Farmer
1967–8	P.N.W. Farmer
	M.G.C. Parry
1968–9	M.G.C. Parry
	S.U. Lamber
1969–70	S.U. Lamber
	R.M. Festing
1970–71	S.U. Lambert
	T.J.P. Ramsden
1971–2	T.J.P. Ramsden
	H.L. Lucas
1972–3	J.R.D. Knox
	M.I.M. Hutchinson
1973	C. Coriat
1974–5	M.R.E. Greenwood
	R.C. Rous
1975–6	O.R.C. Larminie
	E. Foster
	R.S. Burton
1977–8	D.J. Hill
	M.S. Cullen
1978–9	C. Smyth-Osbourne
	A. Kendall
1979–80	C. Smyth-Osbourne
	H. Fayre

BIBLIOGRAPHY

Alma Mater (1815–22). "A Trinity Man." Published 1827.

Sketches of Cantabs (1845). John Smith. Published 1849.

In Cap and Gown. Three Centuries of Cambridge Wit. Edited by Charles Whibley. Published 1889, by Kegan, Paul Trench & Co.

Fores Sporting Notes and Sketches (Volume VIII). Published 1892.

Hunting Reminiscences. Alfred E. Pease, M.P. Published 1898 by W. Thacker & Co.

Half a Century of Sport. Sir Alfred Pease, Bart. Published 1932 by John Lane at The Bodley Head.

The Cambridge Undergraduate One Hundred Years Ago. Oskar Teichman. Published 1926 by W. Heffer and Son Ltd.

Selections of Gunning's Reminiscences of Cambridge. Chosen by D.A. Winstanley. Published 1932 by Cambridge University Press.

Sporting Interludes at Geneva. A. Buxton. Published 1932 by Country Life.

A History of the Fens. J. Wentworth Day. Facsimile of 1954 edition published 1970 by EP Group.

History of the Essex Foxhounds, 1895–1926. Brigadier-General G.D. Bruce. Published 1928 by Vinton & Co.

INDEX

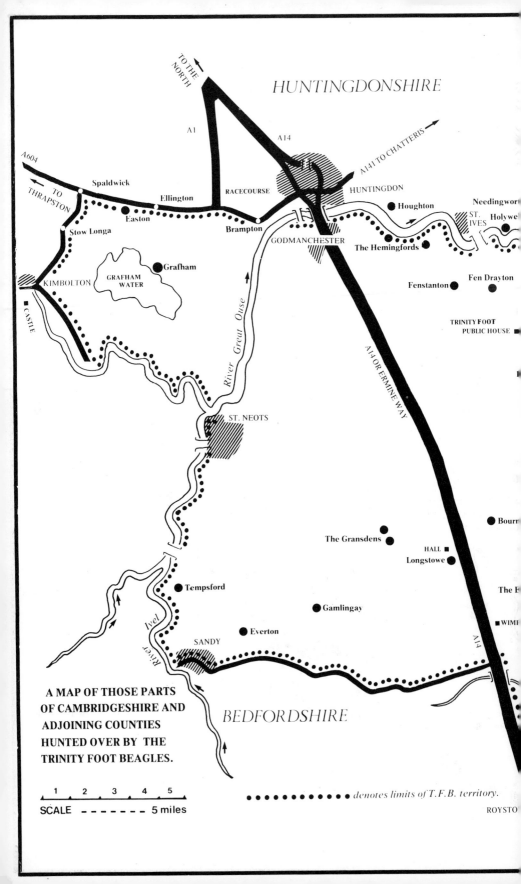

A MAP OF THOSE PARTS
OF CAMBRIDGESHIRE AND
ADJOINING COUNTIES
HUNTED OVER BY THE
TRINITY FOOT BEAGLES.

SCALE ------- 5 miles

•••••••••••••• denotes limits of T.F.B. territory.